THE GOSPEL IN GENESIS

OTHER CROSSWAY BOOKS BY
MARTYN LLOYD-JONES

Alive in Christ

The Cross

The Kingdom of God

My Soul Magnifies the Lord

Out of the Depths

Revival

Seeking the Face of God

True Happiness

Truth Unchanged, Unchanging

Walking with God Day by Day

Why Does God Allow Suffering?

Why Does God Allow War?

Living Water

Let Not Your Heart Be Troubled

GREAT DOCTRINES OF THE BIBLE

Great Doctrines of the Bible (three volumes in one)

LIFE IN CHRIST: STUDIES IN 1 JOHN

Volume 1: *Fellowship with God*

Volume 2: *Walking with God*

Volume 3: *Children of God*

Volume 4: *The Love of God*

Volume 5: *Life in God*

Life in Christ (five volumes in one)

STUDIES IN THE BOOK OF ACTS

Volume 1: *Authentic Christianity*

Volume 2: *Courageous Christianity*

Volume 3: *Victorious Christianity*

Volume 4: *Glorious Christianity*

Volume 5: *Triumphant Christianity*

Volume 6: *Compelling Christianity*

STUDIES IN JOHN 17

The Assurance of Our Salvation (four volumes in one)

THE

GOSPEL IN

GENESIS

From Fig Leaves to Faith

MARTYN
LLOYD-JONES

::: **CROSSWAY** WHEATON, ILLINOIS

Cover design: Josh Dennis

Cover photo: iStock

First printing, 2009

Printed in the United States of America

All Scripture quotations are taken from the King James Version of the Bible.

All emphases in Scripture quotations have been added by the author.

Trade paperback ISBN: 978-1-4335-0120-3

PDF ISBN: 978-1-4335-1257-5

Mobipocket ISBN: 978-1-4335-1258-2

ePub ISBN: 978-1-4335-2079-2

Library of Congress Cataloging-in-Publication Data

Lloyd-Jones, David Martyn.

   The Gospel in Genesis : from fig leaves to faith / Martyn Lloyd-Jones.

      p. cm.

   Includes bibliographical references.

   ISBN: 978-1-4335-0120-3 (tpb)

   1. Bible. O.T. Genesis—Criticism, interpretation, etc. 2. Bible. O.T. Genesis—Relation to the New Testament. I. Title.

BS1235.52.L58   2009

222'.1106—dc22   2009011586

VP		18	17	16	15	14	13	12	11	10	09
14	13	12	11	10	9	8	7	6	5	4	3	2	1

CONTENTS

1

THE MESSAGE OF
THE BIBLE

*Now the serpent was more subtil than any beast of the field
which the LORD God had made. And he said unto the
woman, Yea, hath God said, Ye shall not eat of every tree of
the garden?*

GENESIS 3:1

I call your attention to Genesis 3 in order that we may consider
together the essential message of this book that we call the Bible.
In various ways we have felt the need to do so and have felt it to
be right.

We are all conscious of problems in this world—problems in our
own personal lives and in the world at large. There is no such thing
as complete and perfect happiness. No one is without difficulties.
Everyone knows what it is to be weary, to be disappointed, and to
struggle. We find conflict within ourselves. We find conflict round
and about us. That is the experience of every human being. There
is always a fly in the ointment. There is no such thing as unmixed
pleasure. We have all discovered—and no matter how young we are,
we have discovered this—that life does involve us in difficulties, in
problematical situations. And we have a feeling that we were not
meant for this. We do not like it; we want to be delivered from it.
That is ultimately the cause of all quests in the lives of men and
women. We are all searching for some solution to the problems of

life. There are difficulties; there are such things as heart searchings and disappointments; we are all somehow or other seeking for some way out of some impasse.

We are face-to-face, then, with tribulation and trial, with wretchedness and unhappiness, not only in ourselves but in the world at large. We are always being reminded of this. You cannot pick up a newspaper without seeing it. You never hear the news on the radio without being conscious that life is full of perplexities. Quite apart from major world wars, there is always some misunderstanding and discord, people working at cross-purposes, pulling against one another, rivalries, jealousies, sects and parties. The whole world seems to be nothing but a repetition on a grand scale of what we all experience in our personal lives. That is why it has often been said that man is a sort of microcosm. In and of himself, he is a picture of what is true of the whole cosmos. There seems to be this clash, and as the poet has put it, we see "Nature, red in tooth and claw."[1] There always seems to be struggle—struggle for existence, struggle for power, struggle for mastery.

That is the situation that we meet together to consider, and that in itself is important because many people still think that religion is purely intellectual. Some insist that this book called the Bible, far from being practical, is really very remote from life. They say, if you are interested in the Bible, you can take it up as you take up any other kind of study—music, for instance, or literature—as a kind of hobby. It is something that you do in a detached manner, more or less as a spectator, in your leisure time.

Now all that is a complete fallacy, and I want to try to show you what a terrible fallacy it is. Nothing in the world is as practical as the teaching of the Bible. Indeed, the whole purpose of that book is to come to us with its instruction and its enlightenment concerning the very situation in which we find ourselves. That is what it is for. That is what it is about. From that standpoint, it is in a sense the most human book in the world because from beginning to end it deals with men and women. But for that very reason the Bible is a baffling book to many people. They think of it, as I have said, as just some kind of theoretical textbook offering a certain point of view or line of thought.

Now the Bible does contain massive thought, mighty philosophy, exceptional teaching, and yet the whole time it is also a history book. You cannot get away from men and women—Adam and Eve, Cain and Abel, David and other kings, Jesus of Nazareth, apostles with names, Paul, the servant of Jesus Christ. The Bible keeps on putting its truth to us in terms of these people—what they did, what they said, what happened to them, and so on. And it does that, it seems to me, just to bring home to us this very point that I am emphasizing—that it is a practical book about life. It is a textbook of the soul. It comes to us with a message about the very position in which we find ourselves.

So look at the Bible either as an individual or in terms of the world. Are you unhappy? Is that why you are thinking about what I am saying? Well, the Bible talks to you about your unhappiness. The question is, why are you unhappy? What is the cause of your unhappiness? Why should anybody be unhappy? Why should life not be a perpetual holiday? Why do we have to work by the sweat of our brow? Those are the questions with which the Bible deals. Why do things go wrong? Why is there illness and sickness? Why should there be death? These are the major problems of life.

How important it is that we should realize that this is the starting point. So often when people come to discuss religion they say, "Ah, this is going to be interesting. What about miracles?" And off they go at once. "But science says this and that." And there they are, discussing something far away from themselves, something entirely theoretical. But that is not how the Bible approaches us. The Bible comes to us exactly where we are; it speaks to us in the very position that we are in at this moment. Indeed, it always insists upon doing that. It says, "I am interested in you, and I want to talk to you about yourself."

So we are not going to have a detached, theoretical discussion about some points of philosophy. We are going to talk about you and about me, about all of us in this world and the whole state of the world in which we live. I want to show you what the Bible has to say about all this because in the last analysis there are only two views about life and the world and why things are as they are: we either accept this biblical view, or we accept some other view. These are the classifications that the Bible recognizes—its message and all other messages. I do not care what the other message is. All other messages belong to the same category because they are not based upon the Bible. The Bible is not in a series with the others. It stands absolutely alone. It claims an utter uniqueness. It makes claims for itself that no other book in the world can.

I shall not go into that now because I want to give you the message of the Bible. But were I disposed to do so, I could give you the proofs that the Bible itself provides for its unique and divine inspiration. And on top of that I could give you further proofs that we can deduce from the subsequent course of human history. But for now I am just making the assertion that the only view of men and women and life in the world that really meets the facts, the only view that explains why we are individually as we are at this moment, why the world is as it is and why history has been as it has been, is found in the pages of the Bible. I am here to assert that this book alone has an adequate explanation. If you take up any other view, you will find that it will fail you at some point or other. The Bible, I repeat, claims to be a unique book, a book given by God through men in various ways and brought into one. And what it does, of course, is to give us an account of the things that are vital and primary and fundamental.

Now I want to put all this in general at this point. I am doing this quite deliberately. The Bible is full of a great mass of detail, and my usual custom is to take one verse perhaps, or even less than that, and try to expound it. This is right. We must do that. And yet I believe it is good at times to look at the message as a whole, for I increasingly find that many people have never really seen the whole case put forward by the Bible. They have stumbled at some particular thing; they have stopped at one point. They have missed the whole because they have been over-immersed in one part. They have looked so much at individual trees that they have not seen the forest. So I am going to put this message in terms of the forest, in terms of the general statement of the Bible as it meets us in life as it is today and as it speaks to us. And as I do so, I think we shall see that all along the line the Bible is in blank contradiction to what is so generally and so popularly believed and assumed at the present time.

Certain truths that the Bible tells us are absolute essentials if we are to understand ourselves and the world in which we live. So what does it have to tell us? Well, the whole case is put in the first three chapters of the book of Genesis. We have here the complete biblical view of history and of humanity. We need not go any further; it is all here. So what is it? What am I to make of life? How am I to understand myself, my problems, my disappointments, my unhappiness? How can I face all that? That is the question, is it not? And it is a perfectly fair and right question. But what am I to say about it?

Well, the Bible, in a most extraordinary way, starts like this: "In the beginning God . . ." It starts with God. And at once I have shown you the ultimate distinction with respect to the views that are held about life. Because of necessity, before I begin to ask any questions about myself and my problems, I ought to ask questions like this: Where did the world come from? Where have I come from? What is life itself? What is its origin?

The tragedy of the world today is that it starts too near to its problems. The poet says, "The world is too much with us."[2] That, he says, is our trouble. We are right in the midst of it, and we cannot see it because we are too near it. There are times when to see a thing you must get away from it.

*And what should they know of England
Who only England know?*

Rudyard Kipling, "The English Flag"

If you want to know England truly, travel abroad. If you want to appreciate your own country, go to another. If you simply stay in and walk about the streets of London, in the end you will know very little about London. You need a larger perspective, a distant view. You need to see the thing as a whole. Similarly, do not merely concentrate at once on your problem. Go back. Put it into its context.

To me, that is of the very essence. If you consult mathematicians or chemists—analytical chemists, in particular, or anybody who is having to deal with problems in these realms—and ask them, "How do you tackle a problem?" I think you will find invariably that they will tell you they never start directly with the thing itself. They first of all put it into a group and then into a larger group.

Take a chemist trying to discover what a given substance is. How does he do it? Well, first of all he employs certain broad tests. He eliminates a number of possibilities, and he gradually narrows these down and down and down until he comes to the essential properties of the substance. A physician making a diagnosis has to do exactly the same thing. He must not immediately concentrate on the particular symptom about which the patient is talking. No; the way to discover the cause is to start on a broader base, on a bigger canvas, as it were, and gradually narrow it down. You put certain things out of court and then others.

I once heard a notable physician talking about the way in which he diagnoses a patient. First, he listens to what the patient has to say. Then he examines the patient. So now he has a number of data. He has the patient's symptoms and complaints, and in addition he has his own investigation and discoveries. Then he said, "What I do is this: I say to myself, what are the possible ailments that can include and cover all this? And I put up all the possibilities as though I were putting up a number of pins. Then I stand back and throw several bowling balls at the pins. The pin that's left standing is the right diagnosis." That was his method.

I am trying to tell you that the same method should be applied in the whole question of your particular personal problems and mine.

You come to me and say, "I'm unhappy. I'm conscious of a conflict. I'm in a crisis. What's the matter with me?" And the Bible says, "In the beginning God . . ." as if it has forgotten all about you. But it has not! The only way to understand yourself or your life is to start with God. And right at the very beginning the Bible takes us there. If you are not clear about this, you will go wrong everywhere else.

It is of vital importance to every one of us, therefore, that we know whether or not there is a God. Is everything that exists the result of the activity of God, or is there some blind, impersonal force or energy or power behind everything? Am I face-to-face with a Being and with a Person? Or am I the victim of blind chance, of some accidental meeting of atoms or powers that are without personality, without mind, without reason, without understanding? Is it all blind, or is it all purposeful?

You must come to that. The diagnosis depends essentially upon that. So the Bible, there at the very beginning, starts with that. But the modern panaceas never do that, do they? The psychologist starts with you and ends with you, and so do all the others. They suggest things to you and do certain things to you. They try to bring forces and factors to play upon you. And it is you the whole time. That is why the world is as it is. But you cannot understand life, says the Bible, unless you realize that there, at the back of everything, before everything, is God.

We cannot define God. We cannot understand God. "Canst thou by searching find out God?" (Job 11:7). "The world by wisdom knew not God" (1 Corinthians 1:21). The mightiest Greek philosophers could not attain unto him. But the Bible asserts him. It says this is the revelation that God has given of himself. Now we must agree about this before we can go any further. We either agree that this great eternal God has been pleased to tell us about himself and to reveal and manifest himself—that here is the revelation, and it is in nature and creation also—or else we do not accept it.

The Bible tells us that God is and that God is eternal. Oh, we cannot understand that. Our minds are too small. We cannot conceive of God or eternity. We are so impure that we cannot imagine a Being of whom it can be said, "[he] is light, and in him is no darkness at all" (1 John 1:5) and that he is "a consuming fire" (Hebrews 12:29), that he is absolutely holy in every respect, that he knows all and sees all and is all-powerful. Such truth boggles our minds. We do not understand. We were never meant to understand. If we could, we would be bigger than God. If my mind could go around all these things and I could put them on paper in my little philosophy, I would be god, and God would merely be a subject I am handling.

But the Bible says, "Put off thy shoes from off thy feet, for the place whereon thou standest is holy ground" (Exodus 3:5). We are confronted by one who addresses us with the words, "I AM THAT I AM" (Exodus 3:14)—Jehovah, the eternal God. Now if that is true, it will make a difference all along the line. You cannot reason with blind force. You cannot pray to energy. You cannot put your case and voice your plea to some great impersonal mass. But if God is God, our whole outlook is changed at once. God is personal—"I AM." God is the Father. God is the Son. God is the Holy Spirit. Three Persons in glory. That is the beginning.

But let us go on. The Bible tells us that the world came into being because the eternal God made it. It tells us that God is the Creator. You see, we are still talking about you, are we not? Yes, but we are not just looking at you and your symptoms; we are looking at your whole context. We are asking, where have you come from? How have you come into being? What is it all about?

"Ah," you say, "but what about this pain I want to get rid of?"

Yes, my dear friend, I want to get rid of your pain, but I want to make a diagnosis first. I am not trying to issue an opiate. I do not simply want to give you a drug. We do not gather in church simply to sing and to persuade ourselves that all is well and to feel a little happier. Religion is not escapism. Everything else is escapism, but this is realism. So the Bible tells you that God made the world. It asserts creation. It says that God made everything out of nothing, that he said, "Let there be light: and there was light" (Genesis 1:3). He made everything there is out of nothing by his own power, and he made it perfect. He looked at it, and he saw that it was good, and it was called paradise.

Is the world God's creation, or is it the result of some impersonal, accidental, evolutionary process? I think you can see again how this is a vital matter as we consider our problems in this world. You must believe one or the other of these two ideas. There is no other possibility. Either you believe that God created the world, or you believe the talk that gases—nobody knows how or where they came from—suddenly solidified and formed some primitive slime, and though there is no mind, no understanding, no law, no order, no purpose in anything, somehow or other blind, hidden forces so worked and manipulated and reacted against one another that from a very primitive kind of undefined life they developed into human beings with their brain and power, they produced to the complexity of the flower, the extraordinary instrument that we call the eye, and all the astounding things that happen in creation.

The birds are migrating. They are leaving this country and going back to warmer climes. What makes them do it? Why do they do it? How do they do it? Is it all accident? Is it all chance? Or is there a mind, a Creator, at the back of it all? You see, you cannot begin really to discuss your problems, your personal problems, your personal needs and difficulties, truly and well unless you somehow take all that in. And the Bible makes you do that. It reasons with you. The Bible does not say, "Just come to Jesus and all will be well." Not at all. It starts in Genesis. It starts with creation. It wants you to know and to understand why you are what you are and why God is proposing what he proposes.

So the Bible tells us that the world is not accidental. It tells us that history is not without a beginning. It tells us that there was a time when there was no world and no history and that God deliberately, according to the counsel of his own eternal will, decided to create and form a world and to start the historical process. You and I are in history, and it behooves us to know something about this very process. The Bible asserts that God made the world. It was perfect. It was paradise. He set it going upon its course.

Very well, let us move on. We are coming nearer to ourselves. The next step, of course, is man. We find ourselves members of the human race. Oh yes, I am very concerned about myself. I am an individualist, and I want the solution to my problems. Yes, but I cannot help knowing that there are all these other people like myself in this great world with its teeming masses. "The proper study of mankind is Man."[3] And I am suggesting that it is equally true to say that the proper study of man is mankind. Both propositions are true.

So, then, where do human beings come from? And there again we confront the same great divide. According to the biblical assertion, man is a special creation of God. The Bible tells us, "God created man in his own image" (Genesis 1:27). It does not say that about anything else, only about human beings. In other words, when I am confronting this modern world with all its tragedy and all its pain and all of my own difficulties and problems, I say, what am I, what is man?

Now there was a time when man was perfect. The world was not always as it is now. Man was made in the image of God. Man was made righteous. Man was made holy. He was made *by* God, *for* God. He spoke to God. He walked with God. He communed with God. He enjoyed God. He lived with God. He was upright. There was that in him that could respond to God. And his life was one of perfect bliss.

And in your attempt to understand and solve your problems, you either believe that or else you believe that man, after all, is nothing but an animal—a reasoning animal, if you like, an animal endowed with a higher reason—and that the only difference between him and the other animals is that the forepart of his brain has become more complex, more developed. You believe that man never was perfect and that he is as he is now because he has not yet reached perfection, but he has worked his way up slowly through countless millennia of time—a claim that cannot be proved—until he has arrived at his present state and condition. And you believe that he is slowly improving and developing—he is becoming better, getting rid of things and shedding things that are harmful and inimical to his well-being, and in many, many, many more millennia he will arrive at perfection and will have solved all his problems, and there will be no more troubles.

It is one or the other. You either believe that the human nature you possess has come out of the hands of God and was made by God for himself, or else you take that other view, that purely materialistic view, that man is nothing but an animal. And the Bible, I emphasize, asserts that the second view is wrong. It says that man was made by God and was placed in paradise and there lived his life of perfect enjoyment.

Very well. We now come to the very center of our problem. If all that is true, then why am I what I am? Why is the world what it is? Why the misery and wretchedness? That is our problem, is it not? We have seen what we are, essentially and originally. Why, then, are we what we are now? And here comes the great divide. Notice what the Bible says:

> Now the serpent was more subtil than any beast of the field which the LORD God had made. And he said unto the woman, Yea, hath God said, Ye shall not eat of every tree of the garden? (Genesis 3:1)

People say, "We're not interested in your doctrine." Modern men and women say, "We want a little bit of help. We want a little bit of comfort. Can't you say something to lift us out of our troubles? But there you go, talking theology!"

But, my dear friend, it is only as you believe this theology that you will ever know deliverance. The biblical account of man and of the world and of history is theological, which means that it starts with God. Theology is the science of the knowledge of God, and of all in relationship to God. And this is what theology says at this point—that into this perfect world made by God, in which man lived in a state of paradise, there entered another power, another force. Something came that was opposed to God and opposed to man, and it was bent upon one thing only—wrecking God's perfect work.

Now we come into a realm that no one can possibly understand. And the Bible does not give us ultimate explanations. What it does tell us is that there is a world besides this one, a world that is spiritual, a world of spirits. It tells us that God not only made man but that he made creatures called angels, who are not physical but spiritual beings, and that God endowed them with great and notable and remarkable powers and uses them as his servants. God made these great, powerful, angelic beings. But one of them, we are told, rebelled against God and persuaded others to follow him. He defied God and stood against God, and God smote him, and he fell. And the Bible tells us that this terrible, dread spiritual power, called Satan or the Devil, entered into this world, into God's perfect creation, and by tempting the man and the woman whom God had made brought to pass everything bad that you and I know.

Now let me put that more generally in this way: why are things as they are? Why does any one of us ever desire that which is harmful for us? Why would we ever want to do things that we know to be absolutely wrong? Why are there jealousy and envy and discord and misunderstanding? Why lust and passion? Why are homes and marriages broken? Why do little children suffer? Why all the agony and the pain of life?

That is the problem, is it not? And here is the biblical answer. It is because there is this other power in the world that has dragged man down. There is evil, headed up by this person called Satan, who came and tempted Adam and Eve, and they fell. That is why man is no longer what he once was and has become something entirely different. That is the biblical explanation. You will find it in the Bible from beginning to end. You will find that when the Son of God came into this world, he was tempted by the Devil in the wilderness for forty days. He struggled with him. The Devil tried to get him down. He came and said in essence, "If you are the Son of God, do this, do that. I will give you all the kingdoms of this world if only you will bow down and worship me."

That is what confronts you and me. And if that is true, how hopelessly and utterly inadequate are all the remedies that are being offered apart from the Bible. If that is the problem, if there are these unseen powers, if there are what the apostle Paul calls "principalities . . . powers . . . the rulers of the darkness of this world . . . spiritual wickedness in high places" (Ephesians 6:12), if we are confronted with all that, then we need a power that is greater than that. But the Bible tells us that as the result of that original sin, all of us are in the grip of this evil power. We are dominated by the Devil, "the god of this world" (2 Corinthians 4:4), who comes to us and tempts us.

Have we not all experienced this? The moment you wake up in the morning, before you have had time to start thinking, thoughts come to you. And they are sometimes ugly, foul thoughts, unworthy thoughts. Where have they come from? First thing in the morning, last thing at night, they assault you. You may be reading your Bible, or you may be on your knees in prayer, and you are conscious of being attacked. There are things that drag you down, suggestions and insinuations. Where does it all come from? Here is where it all comes from, says the Bible. And if this is true, how vital it is that you should realize it.

Satan and evil. Original sin and the Fall. We are victims of evil powers greater than ourselves. It is either that, or else you take the other view, so popular today, that the real problem is that man has not had sufficient time to shake off these negative thoughts, that there is still a good deal of the beast in him. He has gone through various stages—fish, reptile, mammal, and so on—and because these animals are creatures of lusts and passions and fight one another and are self-centered and selfish, human beings are still like that. Of course, we are told, we are getting better and every year will continue to get better and better. We are altogether better now than we were two thousand years ago, it is claimed.

"But," you ask, "why are people still fighting?"

"Well," comes the answer, "we haven't had enough time yet."

What about a man coveting another man's wife? Men did that two thousand years ago, and they are still doing it. Where is the improvement? Where is the advance? I do not see it. I see things exactly as they were. I go back and read an early story in the book of Genesis. I see a man named Cain who was so jealous of his brother that he murdered him. I see men still doing that in spite of the fact that probably at least six thousand years have passed.

My friends, the Bible is realistic, is it not? The Bible tells us that we are what we are and things are as they are because of this thing called sin that comes from Satan, that comes from evil, that comes from opposition to God and enmity against God, with man turning himself into a king and a lord and asserting himself. Man's rebellion against God—that is the explanation.

But the Bible goes further and says that man, as the result of all this, is quite helpless, that he has brought a curse upon himself and cannot escape it. He would like to, but he cannot. Man has been trying to get back into Eden ever since he went out of it. That is the whole history of civilization. That is the whole meaning of philosophy and all political thought and all the blueprints of utopias at all times and in all places—man trying to get back into paradise.

But he never will. Why? The flaming sword and the cherubim have been put there by God, and they bar the way! There is also the constant activity of the god of this world, who encourages men and women to try to save themselves because he knows the futility of that and knows it is still nothing but an expression of their self-assertion and opposition to God. So the Devil will encourage godless culture for all he is worth, for while people trust in culture, they will never see their need of the Savior.

But the Bible shows us Adam and Eve thrust out of the garden, miserable, frightened, and alarmed, face-to-face with new problems that were not there before—thorns and thistles, illnesses and diseases, problems on all sides. It has all come upon them. There they are, and they are immersed in it, and they are helpless.

And it is worse than that. Man is under the judgment of God. He thought that he could forget God and that there would be no risk involved. He did not realize that the law of God is absolute. It was there at the beginning, and it is still the same. Both man as an individual and the whole world, according to the Bible, are under the judgment of God. As I understand the Bible, what is happening in the present is that God is manifesting his judgment. He manifested it back there in the garden too. You see, Adam and Eve thought they could eat the forbidden fruit and all would be well. Not at all! Then they heard the voice of the Lord God in the garden in the cool of the evening. God had arrived on the scene, and they cowered and were frightened. Judgment had come, and they were thrust out.

Oh, read your Bible! Read it through, my friend. I am pleading with you. Read your Bible through in the way that I am trying to give you in outline, and you will see how the judgments of God came. They came more than once in the history of mankind. They came at the Flood, upon Sodom and Gomorrah, in the destruction of Jerusalem. And so it has gone on. God is in the heavens, and when man rises up, God judges him. When the people built their Tower of Babel, God smashed it and scattered them, and the result was the division into races and the different languages and so on. There is the history of the world.

Do you see how vital it is to recognize this? I either believe that my life is going on to death and after death the judgment, when I must stand before God, or else I believe that when I come to die, that is just the end, there is nothing more, and when I die it is just like a beast dying, like a flower dying. I have been here, I have gone, and that is all. Can you not see how vital it is to be clear about this matter? Can you not see how it will affect your whole life and all your actions? The Bible asserts that man, though he has turned his back on God, still exists before him.

And it is because of this that I keep preaching. It is because I believe that all who die in their sins not only go to judgment but go to hell that I keep proclaiming the message. If I believed that when

THE GOSPEL IN GENESIS

we all die, that is just the end of it, that our bodies just dissolve and become part of the earth and that is all, then there would be no need of a gospel. But "it is appointed unto men"—all men—"once to die, but after this the judgment" (Hebrews 9:27). Death is not the end. We go on, and we go on for all eternity. The judgment is announced; judgment is pronounced.

But, thank God, man is fallen, condemned, miserable, and helpless, but God intervenes! God comes into the wreckage. God visits man and calls him by name and addresses him. God, even at the moment of rebellion, tells man that he has a way to rescue him and to redeem him: "It [the seed of the woman] shall bruise thy [the serpent's] head" (Genesis 3:15). The serpent, the archenemy, the power with which we cannot deal, the god of this world who is too strong for us, can only be mastered by one, and he has come—the seed of the woman, Jesus of Nazareth, the Son of God. "For God so loved the world, that he gave his only begotten Son, that whosoever believeth in him should not perish, but have everlasting life" (John 3:16). Christ, the Son of God, came into this world, took on our human nature, entered into our very situation, and smote our enemy. He conquered the foe and can set us free. He received judgment for us. He bore our sins and their punishment in his own body on a cruel cross. God dealt with him there and pardons us, and our enemy is conquered. So the way to paradise is open, and it is open for you.

Your misery, all your problems, all your needs, arise from the fact of sin. They arise because you are in this terrible position face-to-face with God. That is the cause of all ill. And there is but one solution to the problem, the solution that God himself has provided in the person of his only begotten Son. ". . . that whosoever believeth in him should not perish, but have everlasting life." And that life begins here and now—a knowledge of God, assurance that you are right with God, that God will bless you and smile upon you and give you what you need, that he will strengthen you and enable you to overcome your enemies, that he will take you through death and announce in the judgment that you are already pardoned and forgiven, that he will say to you, "Well done, thou good and faithful servant . . . inherit the kingdom prepared for you from the foundation of the world" (Matthew 25:21, 34).

My dear friend, that is your problem, and that is the answer to your problem. Believe it. Accept it here and now. Go to that great God, almighty beyond conception and understanding, who existed from eternity and who made all out of nothing. Cast yourself before him. Acknowledge your ignorant, arrogant sinning against him, and thank him for his eternal love in sending his only Son to rescue you and to redeem you by dying for you on Calvary's hill, and ask him to give you life anew. And he will. I say that on the authority of his only Son who stated, "Him that cometh to me I will in no wise cast out" (John 6:37). He cast out man in sin and rebellion. Go back to him in repentance, and he will not cast you out. He will receive you and bless you.

2

GOD AND THE IDEAS OF MAN

Now the serpent was more subtil than any beast of the field which the LORD God had made. And he said unto the woman, Yea, hath God said, Ye shall not eat of every tree of the garden?

GENESIS 3:1

There is no doubt at all that judged from almost any angle you like, Genesis 3 is one of the most important chapters in the entire Bible. That may seem strange to some. Many Christians have felt that surely the whole Old Testament is unnecessary, that as Christians we need nothing but the New Testament. But the early church, which by then was mainly Gentile, decided that the Old Testament should be incorporated with the New Testament in this book that we call the Bible. And undoubtedly these early Christians were guided by the Holy Spirit to do this. They had prayed for guidance, and they believed they had received it. So they said that a Gentile who became a Christian needed the Old Testament just as much as a Jew did. And the reason is that the whole Bible is the history of God's dealing with men and women. It is the history of redemption. And what gives this third chapter of the book of Genesis such exceptional importance is that we are given here the history of how man first fell from the good estate in which God had originally placed him. In other words, it is the beginning of human history.

I say again that I am calling attention to this chapter because we are concerned about a very practical issue. There may have been a time when the preaching of the gospel was a kind of hobby. Some perhaps might even have regarded it as a sort of a luxury. But I do not think anybody can take that view at the present time. Life has become desperate. It is very easy to understand the mentality of our forefathers [in Britain] a hundred years ago. The *pax Britannica* was in vogue. There seemed to be no dangers at all; life went on, and you could make basic assumptions. But it is no longer like that. We in this century and in our generation have come to learn that life is a very critical matter. We have had to learn this, whether we like it or not, and we are concerned about it. We find ourselves surrounded by problems and often overwhelmed by them, and we want to know where we can find relief. What can we do? Is there a way of escape?

Now I was indicating last time, in a very general manner, that the Bible deals with that very situation. There is no more up-to-date book in the world than this old, old book that we call the Bible. It is concerned about men and women. It is concerned about you. It is concerned about all of us just as we are and where we are. It speaks to our very condition and holds before us a way of life. And here in Genesis 3 it tells us why we are in this condition, why things are as they are in the world in general and in our own individual cases. That is the special message of Genesis 3. Let me just remind you of what we have said about this already.

The Bible presents us with a definite, concrete, comprehensive worldview that is absolutely different from anything you can find anywhere else. The great marks, I said, of its message are these: it starts with God; it tells us that he has created everything; it tells us that man is not merely an evolving animal but a special creation of God; it tells us how Satan and evil came in, how man fell, how man is utterly helpless and under the judgment of God. But it tells us also how God in his infinite love and mercy and compassion has intervened and has provided a great and a grand way of salvation, which is preached and offered to the human race.

That is our general statement, and we are given all that in just one chapter. But the point I want to make now is that this is actual history. This is something that literally did happen. I must not dwell on this subject too long, and yet it is very important. There are people who say, "Yes, I'm interested in Christian doctrine, but I'm not interested in those early chapters of Genesis." That is an utterly illogical position. I cannot see how anybody can believe in the Christian salvation taught in the New Testament without believing these chapters of Genesis.

One of the greatest exponents of the Christian faith that the world has ever known was the mighty apostle Paul, and he tells us that we are as we are because of the sin of Adam and that we all sinned with him and we all fell with him. And Paul says that over against Adam is the Lord Jesus Christ: "For as in Adam all die, even so in Christ shall all be made alive" (1 Corinthians 15:22). The first man did this; the second man did that.

It is very important, therefore, that we should be glad that this is history. This is what makes the Bible such an extraordinary book and fills it with such fascination. I repeat that Genesis 3 is first of all history. But in addition to being history, it is an actual account of what every one of us does. According to the Bible, the remarkable thing about men and women in sin is that not only have they been taken down, as it were, by Adam, but they do the very selfsame thing themselves. They go on repeating the action of Adam. So here we have this amazing history, and at the same time we are given an analysis of the very thing that we do ourselves.

Let me put it like this: we find Adam and Eve becoming desperately miserable, filled with a sense of fear, and hiding, not knowing what to do with themselves. We find them condemned to a certain type of life, with the woman told that she will have to bear her children in sorrow and in pain, and the man told that he must work and earn his bread by the sweat of his brow. There they are in that condition. Now the question is, how did they ever get into that state? Remember, they were not always like that. Go back to Genesis 2, and you will find there they were in a condition that is described as paradise. Yet now here they are in this abject misery. What produced this tremendous change?

And the answer is given in the first verse of Genesis 3. It was because man ceased to listen to God and to what God said. There is really nothing more to say than that. That is the proposition. There is only one explanation as to why the world is as it is at this minute and as to why every single individual is as he or she is at this second. It is that the man and the woman listened to that question of the tempter: "Hath God said . . . ?" That is, "Do you really believe that? Are you really being bound by that?" The Devil came and said, "Hath God said, Ye shall not eat of every tree of the garden?" And because they accepted that question and acted upon it, they brought ruin upon themselves and upon all their posterity.

And this, I want to show you, is the perfect picture of every one of us. There you see Adam and Eve confronted by God's way—God had made them; God had blessed them; God had surrounded them with benefits and put them in the garden, in paradise. They simply had to pick the fruit, as it were, and enjoy themselves and enjoy their communion with God. Yes, they did all that. But God added something to that. God added a law. God said to them in effect, "You can go on living this sort of life endlessly—on one condition." And the condition was that they obeyed God, that they recognized the supreme authority of God, that they recognized that God had a right to do with his own as he chose and that God really, even in giving his law, was concerned about their well-being and happiness. That was the position. The blessings were being showered upon them, but there was this law, this condition, this demand for obedience. But they rejected that. It was just at that point that they went wrong and brought all that misery upon themselves.

Now the whole case for the gospel of Jesus Christ today is just like that. I preach because God has spoken. He has spoken to the world. He has sent his only Son into this world to speak to us and to give us a message. What is it? Well, God offers to take us as his children, to make us his heirs. He offers all the fullness of his own blessed Son and the blessings of the gospel, which Paul describes as "the unsearchable riches of Christ" (Ephesians 3:8). He offers us the kind of life that Christ himself lived, a life of joy and peace and many wondrous unmixed blessings. But he adds to it the same demand, the same request. He would have us live as the Lord Jesus Christ lived. He would have us be holy. He says, in offering us all these blessings of the gospel, "Be ye holy; for I am holy" (1 Peter 1:16).

The gospel of Jesus Christ, in other words, is not just some pleasant message that says, "Go and do anything you like; God loves you. It will be all right at the end. Receive all these blessings, and there's no more to say." God does not stop at that. "Ye that love the LORD," says the psalmist, "hate evil" (Psalm 97:10). If you want to love God, the gospel tells us, you cannot love mammon at the same time. If you want to walk along the narrow way, you cannot continue on the broad way. If you want your house to be on a rock, it cannot be on the sand.

Always coupled with the blessings, there is this demand. The gospel is not just a statement that God is benevolent and loving and that it does not matter what we do, that everything will be all right at the end because God is love. And because it is not that, men and women still object and still go on repeating exactly what was done in the garden at the beginning by Adam and Eve.

I want to try to show you, therefore, as we look at these first verses in this third chapter of the book of Genesis, what exactly we do when we reject Christ. There is something almost unbelievable about this story, is there not? As we look at it in terms of Adam and Eve, we find it almost incredible that they could have done such a thing. But they did. I say again that this is history, and all the consequences have followed. And I am holding the picture before you, I repeat, because it is an equally true portrayal of what every one of us has done. Oh, that we may have grace to see it! If we could only see ourselves as we are in sin, I do not believe we would stay there

THE GOSPEL IN GENESIS

another second. And God, in his grace, has given us a picture so that we may see exactly what we are doing.

The first point that I observe as I look at this picture is the way in which this rebellion began. What was it that made Adam and Eve behave as they did? What was it that led them to eat of that prohibited fruit? Well, the astounding thing is that they did it simply on the strength of the dogmatic assertion of the Devil, and because of nothing else whatsoever. I wonder if you have ever noticed that as you have considered this chapter. Have you seen that the Devil did not give any reasons at all? I see it all in the original question: "Yea," he asked, "hath God said, Ye shall not eat of every tree of the garden?" And you hear the sneer in his voice. His whole philosophy comes out at once. He is raising a query. "Poor innocents," he seems to say, "do you really believe that?" He does not provide any proofs at all. He simply asserts certain things. He puts it still more specifically later: "Ye shall not surely die" (Genesis 3:4). And that is all there is to it: "I say so!" And they listened.

Now it is at that point that I find it rather difficult at times to understand Adam and Eve. And yet the moment I begin to think, I understand them very well because I know that everybody who is a sinner—and we are all sinners by nature—and everybody who remains in sin is in that position in exactly the same way.

Now this is rather striking, is it not? Have you ever realized that people who are not Christians are really basing their whole position simply upon nothing else but a dogmatic assertion? There is no proof whatsoever. Of course, I know that people say, "*Science proves . . .*" But does science prove? "Of course," they say, "no sensible person, nobody who has any learning, especially any scientific knowledge, believes that today." And because somebody comes to me with that assertion, I am expected to say that I had better not believe. But nothing has been proved at all. And yet we say, "All right, we will turn our backs and say we no longer believe."

That is the very thing that Adam and Eve did. They listened to a dogmatic pronouncement unaccompanied by any proof whatsoever.

And this is where the contradiction emerges. People are never tired of speaking of the dogmatism of the pulpit—the dogmatism of the preacher, the dogmatism of the church—and they do not like it. But I want to ask you a simple question: if you are not a Christian, if you do not believe the Bible and if you do not believe in God, on what grounds are you not believing? What are your reasons? What is your argument? Where is your proof? Can you prove to me that there is no God? Can you prove to me that Jesus of Nazareth was not the only begotten Son of God with two natures in one person? You say you do not believe it. You do not believe in miracles either. Does that prove that he never worked a miracle? Can you prove it? Do you have anything beyond a dogmatic assertion?

I have often quoted a famous statement made about a hundred years ago by Matthew Arnold, a very literary man, but I want to quote it again because I think it is a perfect example of the attitude to which I am referring. He put it like this: "Miracles cannot happen. Therefore, miracles have not happened." There is no more to say, in his view. And people listen to that, and they still believe it. Matthew Arnold says it all: "Miracles cannot happen. Therefore, miracles have not happened." Of course, if the first statement is right, the second is right, and the "therefore" is perfectly legitimate. But the vital question is, what about the first statement? Who can establish the fact that miracles cannot happen? Nobody can. It has never been done; it never will be done.

Now I must not stay with this preliminary method, but, my dear friend, I do trust that I am opening your eyes to this position. What are the grounds of your unbelief? What is the basis for your rejection of the gospel? What do you really have to substantiate what you say you believe and what you do not believe? On what is it actually based? Do you have anything to say except "So and so does not believe . . ." or "I read an article" or "I heard a man say . . ." or "Nobody any longer believes . . ." or "Science says . . ." and so on and so forth? I suggest to you that when you analyze your unbelief, you will find that it just comes to that. It is a tremendous hoax.

I take the view of those who say that the greatest hoax of the last hundred and fifty years has been the theory of evolution. It has hoaxed the vast majority of people. It was originally a theory, but it has been turned and twisted as if it were a fact that everybody believes. But it is pure dogmatic assertion. It is nothing beyond a supposition.

That happened at the beginning, and it has been happening ever since. On the basis of a pure bit of dogmatism, man has brought upon himself the misery and the wretchedness that he is still enduring. Let me appeal to you in the name of Christ and of the gospel, begin to think. Think! "That's all sob stuff," you say. This is not sob stuff. The great appeal of the gospel is to men and women to think. They have been duped by the Devil. They are living in darkness.

When the risen Lord commissioned the apostle Paul to go out preaching and to be a witness to the people, he said, "Open their eyes . . . turn them from darkness to light, and from the power of Satan unto God" (Acts 26:18). Go and enlighten them, said Christ to Paul. Open their eyes. Teach them. Instruct them. Make them think. Tell them how to think. Men and women are deluded by a prejudice; they are silenced by a dogmatism that comes from the archenemy. It began like that, and it has continued like that. That is the trouble.

But now let us observe some of the steps of the process, the stages through which the man and woman went after they were bemused by the dogmatism of Satan, this shining personality who came in the form of a serpent and dazzled them by his authority, just as so many are dazzled today by the authority of big names and science and other abstractions.

First, as a result of listening to the serpent, the man and woman began to doubt God's power. The Devil said:

> Yea, hath God said, Ye shall not eat of every tree of the garden? And the woman said unto the serpent, We may eat of the fruit of the trees of the garden: but of the fruit of the tree which is in the midst of the garden, God hath said, Ye shall not eat of it, neither shall ye touch it, lest ye die. And the serpent said unto the woman, Ye shall not surely die. (Genesis 3:1–4)

"Don't believe it," said the Devil. "When God spoke to you like that, it sounded very powerful, but you need pay no attention. You can eat of that fruit, and I assure you that you shall not die. God can't do anything about it. It's an idle word. Don't listen to it. Don't be frightened. Don't be tyrannized. Stand up against him. It's not true."

So they began to question the power of God. That was the first step. And it is always the first step. If we just realized the power of God, we would not continue defying him for a second. It is because of this doubt, this unbelief, that people still continue in sin. The Bible states the alternative like this: "The fear of the LORD is the beginning of wisdom" (Psalm 111:10). "It is a fearful thing," says another Scripture, "to fall into the hands of the living God" (Hebrews 10:31). Remember, too, the message that was given by the prophet Daniel to King Belshazzar at his feast. Daniel pointed out that not only had Belshazzar desecrated the vessels of the temple by drinking from them with his concubines, but even more serious, said Daniel, "The God in whose hand thy breath is, and whose are all thy ways, hast thou not glorified" (Daniel 5:23). The moment Adam and Eve began to doubt the power of God, everything else followed.

And this method, this process, is still being repeated. The Bible is full of it. Take even a man like Moses. When Moses was first called by God to his task, he had that great vision of the burning bush. He was about to go forward and investigate when back came the voice saying to stand back. "Put off thy shoes from off thy feet, for the place whereon thou standest is holy ground" (Exodus 3:5).

Oh, the power of God! Has it ever occurred to you that the very way in which we tend to talk about God is in and of itself an expression of our denial of the power of God? How fond we are, all of us, of religious debates and discussions. What is more enjoyable than to have an argument about these matters? Someone will say, "I don't see that God can do this or that." There the man is, perhaps standing with his hands in his pockets and a cigarette in his mouth, talking about God. But God said to Moses in effect, "Take your shoes off. Do you realize who I am and what I am? I AM WHAT I AM. Are *you* coming to investigate *me*? Stand back!"

He is the true God, the Creator of the ends of the earth, everlastingly almighty in his eternity and in his glory, who never knows what it is to be weary or to be tired, who never faints. And yet think of the way in which all of us have spoken about him and have argued about him and have expressed our opinions about him. There is no fear of God before our eyes. That is the trouble. We do not know what we are speaking about. We do not understand God.

And then, of course, with our characteristic modern confidence, we smile at strong biblical preaching and say, "Of course, our forefathers a hundred years or so ago could be frightened, you know. And as long as people were subject to this spirit of fear, they were Christians and believed the gospel. We're familiar with all that. Since then we've studied the science of comparative religion, and we know that all these religions are based upon fear, with God as some sort of great bogeyman in the heavens. And people are ready to believe it. Some believe the same things about the sun and others about the moon and the stars. Comparative religion teaches us all this. Today we know too much to be taken in by that sort of thing! 'Has God said?' Fancy, people being frightened in that way! Fancy, people being alarmed about hell! Fancy, people crying out in fear and trembling, 'What must I do to be saved?' We've lost that superstitious fear of God."

I am not drawing a caricature, am I? Am I not speaking the sober, literal truth? Is not that the attitude of men and women toward this almighty God at this very moment? They are defying God. They are defying his power. A man says:

> *My head is bloody, but unbowed....*
> *I am the master of my fate:*
> *I am the captain of my soul.*
>
> William Ernest Henley,
> "Invictus. In Memoriam R. T. H. B."

I, modern man, am self-sufficient. I will stand and defy what-ever gods there may be. I cannot be frightened. I cannot be tyrannized. I cannot be alarmed. I'm not afraid of death. I'm not afraid of eternity. I'm not afraid of God.

This attitude may not always be expressed in those words, but if your life is not entirely submitted to God, that is your position. For if you really believe in the power of God over and above you, you will fall at his feet. You will prostrate yourself. You will look into his face and say, "Have mercy upon me. Bless me." Are you doing that? Have you ever? Who is controlling your life and your ideas? Is it God, or is it you yourself and the modern world? Doubt came in about the power of God.

But still more serious, the Devil insinuated a doubt about the goodness of God. Do you remember how he put it? The Devil said to those first two people, "For God doth know that in the day ye eat thereof, then your eyes shall be opened, and ye shall be as gods, knowing good and evil" (Genesis 3:5).

"You know," said the Devil to Adam and Eve in effect, "I've felt sorry for you for a long time. I've seen the way God has frightened you and tyrannized over your life, and I've been wanting to tell you the truth, and I've come to do that. Do you know why he said all this about the fruit? Well, he doesn't want you to become what you ought to be and what you have it in you to be. You see, he's jealous, and he doesn't want you to become gods and to know good and evil as he does. So he told you not to eat of that fruit because the moment you do eat it, you will be like God himself. That's why he's introduced this prohibition."

And they believed it! They began to doubt the justice and the righteousness of God, the benevolence of God, the goodness of God. They began to doubt—I do not hesitate to put it like this—the very morality of God. They listened to the Devil when he told them that God was against them and that was why he had introduced the prohibition. They believed that God was jealous and selfish and small and was keeping things from them in order to lord it over them.

I probably do not need to point out to you that this is the appalling thing that millions of people are believing about God at this very moment. In their heart of hearts they regard God as a monster, someone who is against them, someone who delights in spoiling their lives. Are those not the common grounds that are brought forward for refusing to believe the gospel?

I wonder whether I am addressing any young person who perhaps has left home for the first time. So far you have been taken to a place of worship by your parents, but now you have left home and have come to London. Do you have thoughts like this in your heart? "I'm going to give this Christianity stuff up. It's held me down; it's robbed me of so much, this narrow life, chapel-going, reading the Bible, prayer meetings, and so on." Perhaps you are saying, "I've missed so much. At last I have my opportunity. Now I'm really going to start living and enjoying life."

We have all known this. We have had a feeling that the gospel is something narrow and cramped that puts fetters upon us and robs us of some marvelous life that the people who have not been brought up like us have always enjoyed. Is that not the thought? That somehow God and this Christian way of life are against us and are opposed to our best interests and to our enjoyment of life and to our happiness, and that somehow or other God does not wish us well or desire us to enjoy our lives in this world. That is still the idea, is it not? And coupled with that, of course, is the notion that God's judgment is wrong, that it is unfair, and that God has no right to speak like this to us. Why should I stand in the judgment at the end? Doubting God's goodness is the second step.

Now notice the next step—how interesting these steps are, and how we all repeat them as we go through life in this world! The next step was inevitably this one: human reason came in and substituted itself for God's way. Do you see the steps? Starting from the dogmatism, the assertion, first there was the questioning of God's power and then the questioning of God's goodness. Next came the thought, "Well, after all, there's something in this." It is put like this in the sixth verse: "And when the woman saw that the tree was good for food"—she had always seen that tree, it had been there before she came there, she had often looked at it, but she had never seen this before—"and that it was pleasant to the eyes, and a tree to be desired to make one wise, she took of the fruit thereof, and did eat."

That is always the next step. We start with a query about the power of God. We say, "We needn't be afraid. We really mustn't be cowards. We mustn't allow these feelings and fears to dominate us. We must shake that off and stand on our feet." And then we say, "Well, let's examine this God. Is he good? No, no. Why, that religion is too small. It's too narrow. The other is so much bigger." But the moment you get there, you begin to reason and to work out your own philosophy, and you say, "Well, of course, I've always been brought up to think that the worldly life is a very bad life. But really, now that I come to look at it, it doesn't seem to be so bad. Look at the people who are living it. They don't die the moment they sin. They seem to be able to do anything they like, and they flourish on it. They look much happier than many of those miserable Christians. My word, this isn't a bad life after all! And look at the great people who are living such a life. Look at the publicity they get!"

And then, of course, we say, "Well, we don't want to give up religion altogether. What shall we do? Well, let's make a religion that's more satisfactory." And so, by exercising our human reason and our own thoughts, we begin to create a new god. "Oh, yes," we say, "we want to believe in God, but not a God with prohibitions, not a God with a law, not a just and a righteous and a holy God, not a God who stands in judgment and threatens us with hell. No, no. The God we want, the God we believe in, is a God who is always smiling upon us and who says, 'It's all right, I'll forgive everything. Carry on.'"

Is that not what is being done? Put down on paper your ideas of God, what you think God is like and what God ought to be, and compare them with the Bible, and I think you will find that I have not exaggerated by a single syllable. Having come to this stage, men and women now forget God altogether and substitute their own opinions, their own philosophy. And that is what has been happening for a hundred years. The Bible is no longer the authority. We no longer listen to God; we are listening to human beings.

But there is something here that to me is more amazing and more astonishing than all this, and it is the fact that men and women can do this in spite of what God has done for them and in spite of all the blessings they have enjoyed. That is what I meant when I said at the beginning that there is a sense in which I just do not understand it.

Have you ever thought of it like that? Look at this man Adam. Look at Eve. Think of what God had done for them. He had made them. He had given them everything. He had made them lords of creation. He had given them this marvelous life in paradise. He would come to speak to them. He would visit them. They were walking with him. They were enjoying bliss that passes our imagination. Everything was easy. Everything was perfect. God had done all that for them. And yet they were ready and willing to believe all these lies about him, to turn their backs upon him, to disobey him, and thus to bring down all this upon their heads.

Do you not find it difficult to understand that? What is it, you say, about a man who lets down a friend? What do you say about the sort of man, let us call him A, who was in serious and terrible trouble and his friend B helped him, gave him money, allowed him to share his house, showered gifts upon him, did everything he could for him without skimping at all? What do you think of that man A who is ready to listen to some foul insinuation that is made against his friend B? Someone comes and tells him, "Look here, he did that because it was to his advantage to do it, because it benefited him. He wasn't doing it for your sake. He always thinks of himself; he's selfish and self-centered. Fancy believing that he did it out of the goodness of his heart and out of his own benevolence! Did you really believe that? It isn't true!"

And *A* believes those lies and repeats them, and he does things against his greatest friend and benefactor. What would you think of him? You would call him a cad, would you not? And you would be right.

So what do you say about Adam and Eve? It was in spite of what God had done for them and all the blessings he had showered upon them that they believed the lie and resented him and, as it were, turned their backs upon him and went their own way. But, my dear friend, that is precisely what everybody who is not a Christian at this moment is still doing. It is God who has given you life. It is God who saw to it that you should be born into a family with loved ones who would care for you and look after you. It is God who ordained marriage. It is God who ordained the family. It is God who ordained the state. It is God the Father who sends the rain. It is God who gives the sun. It is God who fructifies the crops in the fields and gives us food. Do you know that he could stop it all in a second if he chose to do so? It is God in his beneficence who does all this. It is Providence that has surrounded us with all these glorious gifts and benefits from our very birth into this life.

Not only that, have you ever stopped to think of the benefits of Christianity in a general sense that you have enjoyed? Has it ever occurred to you that many of the things you prize most of all in this world have come as by-products of the Christian faith? Your education and hospitals, for instance—Christianity introduced them. They would never have come but for Christianity and the church. The world would never have provided them. Do not believe my word; go back into history. Trace it for yourselves. And you have enjoyed them. They have come from God. He has showered them upon you.

But all this pales into insignificance by the side of something else that God has done. "For God so loved the world, that he gave his only begotten Son, that whosoever believeth in him should not perish, but have everlasting life" (John 3:16). God so loved this world that had rebelled against him and spat into his face that in spite of that he sent his only Son, and that Son—I do not understand it—came and was born as a baby in Bethlehem. He humbled himself, he went to the cross, he died on a tree so that you and I might be redeemed, forgiven, and restored to God and go to heaven. And yet men spat in his face. They still do.

The old action of Adam and Eve is repeated today. In spite of all that God had done for them, they believed the lie, and men and women still believe the lie. They have looked at Calvary, they have looked at the cross, and they have said, "It's not true. God is against us." The God who did that is against us? There is only one thing to say about that. It is madness, my friends. You are being beguiled. You are being bemused. Dust has been thrown into your eyes. Can you not see the folly of it all? To say that a God who did that and did not spare his only Son is selfish and arrogant and waiting to crush you and is against you! Face the facts. Recognize the unutterable folly of such an attitude. If you do not realize it now, a day will come when you will know that all this is true.

The Devil looked at Adam and Eve and said, "Don't believe it. Eat the fruit—eat as much as you like. You shall not surely die." But they did die. Death came into the world, and it has been here ever since.

"No evil consequences will follow," said the Devil. But they did—the man and woman were turned out of paradise; food had to be earned by the sweat of their brow. Is that not true? We do not like it. We are trying to fight against it. A seven-day week, a six-day week, a five-day week. If we could have it, we would want a no-day week! Permanent holidays! Everything for nothing.

"In the sweat of thy face shalt thou eat bread" (Genesis 3:19). Painful childbirth was another consequence. It all came, it is all still here, and it will all continue.

"Ye shall not surely die." But as a result, Adam and Eve were driven out, working, sweating, bearing children in pain, murder coming in among those very children, death. How easy it is to make dogmatic pronouncements with nothing to substantiate them, but they make not the slightest difference to the truth about God.

You and I at this moment are in the presence of this almighty and eternal God. Do you not feel that it is time to take off your shoes and to put your hand on your mouth and to be careful of what you say? We are in his hand. He has made his way plain and clear. He has shown us why the misery has come upon us, and he offers us the only way out. There is full, free salvation at this very moment in Jesus Christ. You have but to realize the truth and to acknowledge to God that all your troubles are due to your sin, your rebellion against him. Go and tell him that. Tell him that you receive his offer in Christ. If you do that, he will receive you, and he will bless you. The wrath of God will no longer abide upon you. You need no longer fear death and the grave. You need not fear God. You will know that you have been reconciled to him and that you have become his child.

In other words, reverse the process that happened in the garden. Then all will be well with your soul. Give up your foolish reasoning, and listen to God. Believe his word. Submit yourself to it. And soon you will delight in it, for you will be living the life of God himself.

Instead of asking, "Has God said?" say, "I believe what God has said. I accept it. I surrender to it." Do that and you will be blessed in a manner that you will never understand in this world. You will be blessed even in the act of death, and you will go on to be with God and with Christ throughout eternity.

3

FIG LEAVES

And the eyes of them both were opened, and they knew that they were naked; and they sewed fig leaves together, and made themselves aprons. And they heard the voice of the Lord God walking in the garden in the cool of the day: and Adam and his wife hid themselves from the presence of the Lord God amongst the trees of the garden. And the Lord God called unto Adam, and said unto him, Where art thou?

GENESIS 3:7-9

This third chapter of Genesis, let me remind you, is absolutely vital to a true understanding of the message of the entire Bible. We meet together in a Christian church to consider this message. The church is not a philosophical society, nor a cultural society. Its business is to expound and to proclaim the message of this book. It is not interested, primarily, in anything else. That is why a meeting, a service, at church is unique. All services thus held in the name of Christ are unique in the sense that we start by making the claim that we come from God with a message from him. We do not start with ourselves. We are not involved in an endeavor to arrive at God or at anything else. We come to consider a message from God.

There is a great message in this book, a message for men and women as they are at this moment. It is not far away from or divorced from life but is the most practical message in the world. This book has spoken to generation after generation. It came to them exactly where they were and as they were, and that is precisely what it does still. It is not dealing with some theoretical question or interest. There are such books, and they have their place, their importance, but that is not what we have here. The Bible tells us throughout that we only pass through this world once. But it also tells us that we are determining at the same time our eternal and everlasting future and that, therefore, this is the most vital matter that we can ever consider.

All along the Bible presents its truth to us in this way: it reminds us that we must do something about it. It is always impressing upon us the urgency of the position. If you are interested in the technical terms, it always presents its truth in an *existential* manner, and that means that I cannot afford to sit back and consider it casually in a detached way. The Bible says you cannot do that because you are in an uncertain world, and your whole life is uncertain. And, therefore, it always appeals to us to give it great attention.

The Bible is here to deal with the problems that confront each one of us. It is here to talk to us about ourselves. Genesis 3:9 reminds us of that. It tells us, "The LORD God called unto Adam, and said unto him, Where art thou?" This is a direct and personal address. God is speaking to us. He is speaking to us individually. He is speaking to us about where we are, why we are there, how we ever got there, how we can come from there. That is its whole message. In other words, its interest is in us, in our problems, our pains, our perplexities, our troubles, and all the things that tend to make life so difficult.

And I am saying that if we really are to understand the message of the Bible, we must understand the message of this third chapter of Genesis, because it is foundational. This is the chapter in which we are told exactly why things are as they are. This chapter is historical.

"But," you say, "that's an assertion."

I agree. I cannot prove it to you as one can prove a mathematical problem, but the greatest things in life cannot be proved in that sense. I could suggest many things to you that you take for granted and that you know to be true but that you cannot prove in a mathematical sense. The whole case of this book, the Holy Bible, is that it is historical. It is the explanation of why people are as they are. But in addition to that, as I indicated earlier, in a very remarkable manner Scripture also describes us one by one as we are now. That is the extraordinary thing about human beings and sin. All of us, as it were, in addition to inheriting certain things, repeat what was done at the beginning by Adam and Eve.

In the previous study we were looking at that from the point of view of the intellect. Man has fallen and has gone astray in every respect, and he started with his mind. He accepted the Devil's dogmatic statement, and as he began to look at it and to fondle it, he liked it. And in spite of all that God had done for him, he accepted what Satan told him about God's character and God's power, and he deliberately rebelled against God. He accepted another point of view, and he acted upon it. And then he began to reap the consequences. And we will show that man is still doing that—he is ready to swallow the most dogmatic assertions that lack any vestige of proof whatsoever because they have great names attached to them and because they are made with a great show of certainty.

It is not only Christians who point this out about modern thinking. I think of a radio lecture on the theme of what was called "humbug in science." It was a most interesting address and perfectly true. It showed how people, even scientists, can, and do, mislead themselves in various ways. That is universally true, but it is particularly true in the realm of science. Man still defies God and rebels against him merely on the basis of some theory or some dogmatic statement, and then he repeats the whole sorry process. He displays his doubts of God, his hatred of God. He reveals his ingratitude toward God. He uses his own reason and substitutes it for divine revelation. You remember how we are told that when the woman saw that the tree was good for food and that it was pleasant to the eyes, she started using her own understanding and her own reason. And so she took the fruit and ate it. It is the selfsame process. It happened there at the beginning, and it is still being repeated.

THE GOSPEL IN GENESIS

But now I want to show you that not only is this being done in the realm of the intellect and understanding, it is being repeated in a much more experiential, a much more practical, manner. It is what man in sin is constantly doing, and here we have a perfect description of it. I confess again that I find this difficult at times, and if I did not know that this biblical teaching about sin is true and that the god of this world blinds our minds, I would be altogether at a loss to understand it. I find it difficult to understand how it is possible for anybody really to read this third chapter of Genesis and not at once to recognize that here we have nothing but a perfect description and delineation of what has been true of every one of us. It is astounding to me that anybody could read that book and not say, "That must be true because that is exactly what I've been and what I've done. It's an account of me; it's an account of men and women as I see them in the world today."

But, of course, instead of doing that, we try to explain the facts away in terms of psychology and in various other ways, as I hope to indicate. And so the voice of God falls upon deaf ears, and men and women, immersed in sorrows and problems and trials and tribulations, refuse the one thing that can deliver them and give them salvation. That is the muddle to which sin always leads. That is what happens to us when we refuse to listen to God and go our own way. We have brought ourselves into trouble. We even refuse the help that is offered to bring us out of it. And so we go on and on, turning round and round in circles and never reaching the point at which we would like to arrive.

So let me remind you of these facts. Man, in the way we have seen, rebels against God, and then certain consequences follow. What are they? Well, they are described here as they happened at the beginning to Adam and Eve. And as we consider them, I think you will see that they are an accurate description of what is still happening. "The woman . . . did eat, and gave also unto her husband with her; and he did eat." And then at once "the eyes of them both were opened, and they knew that they were naked; and they sewed fig leaves together, and made themselves aprons" (Genesis 3:6–7).

What does this mean? Well, the first consequence of this act of rebellion and sin was this: they at once became conscious of a loss. There is a very interesting phrase here: "The eyes of them both were opened, and they knew that they were naked." What does that mean? Nobody knows exactly, but at any rate it does suggest, does it not, that they were conscious at once that they were deprived of something that they'd had before. They knew that they were in some sense naked; before they had not been naked. What is this? I do not know, but I am inclined to agree with those who suggest, as an exposition of this, that man at the beginning, as he was made perfect by God, had a kind of glory about his body even as there was about his soul. Man, when he fell, not only fell in his spirit, but he also fell in his body. The apostle Paul tells us that at the end, when our Lord comes again, "[He] shall change our vile body"—the body of our humiliation—"that it may be fashioned like unto his glorious body"—the body of his glorification (Philippians 3:21).

Man, let us remember, was made in the image of God in every respect. He was not only upright with a righteousness that was spiritual, but there was, I believe, a glory pertaining to the body. And when Adam and Eve sinned, they lost that glory and were left with bodies as we now know them, and they were aware that they had been deprived of something. There was immediately a consciousness of a nakedness, a loss, an incompleteness. Something had gone. A glory had departed.

And that, I suggest to you, has been the simple truth about men and women ever since. There is nothing more obvious than that every one of us has a sense of loss. Do we not all have an idea that somehow or other we are missing something? We all have an idea that there is something better, something higher. We all know something about a longing for what Wordsworth has called "an ampler ether, a diviner air."[4] You cannot explain it away. You have this sense; everybody has it. Every single person, it does not matter how far sunk in sin in an obvious, external manner, somehow has this idea that there is a better possibility. There is something more somewhere. That is why all the modern analyses, which are not based upon the Bible, are so shallow and incomplete.

What is the meaning of this restlessness that is in human nature? What is the meaning of this constant search for something that we do not have and that we do not seem able to find? Upon what is it all based? There is only one adequate answer. We have an innate feeling that we were meant for something bigger and higher. There is in every one of us a recollection, a memory, of what we once were. We were all in Adam. Man was made perfect in the image of God. He was upright; he was righteous. There was glory about his very body. And though we have lost this and though we have never known it, a memory lingers. It is in the whole of human nature. It is in all humanity, a sense of something else.

Of course, people have tried to interpret this in other ways, and they have gone wrong in doing so. Plato tried to explain it, and Wordsworth borrowed his idea when he said:

Trailing clouds of glory do we come
From God, who is our home.

Wordsworth believed that we start in this world with the glory still, but then:

Shades of the prison-house begin to close
Upon the growing Boy.

William Wordsworth,
"Ode. Intimations of Immortality"

Man had it at the beginning, but somehow he lost it.

Well, actually he had lost it long before that. He lost it before he came into this world. But the memory remains, and the Platonic idea is simply an attempt somehow to explain this recollection, this sense we have within us that we were meant for something bigger and higher, that we are being deprived of something. We all have this idea that we were meant for happiness, that we were meant for peace, that we were meant for a life of joy, but that somehow this has been taken from us. And thus men and women are ever restless, ever ill at ease, and find it difficult to live with themselves and with others.

And in Genesis, at the very beginning, we are given this extraordinary description of this loss. It is in a pictorial form, but it is true nevertheless. Shall I put that in a personal form before I pass on to my second question? Are you not aware of this sense of incompleteness? Is there not some kind of urging within your being that is crying out for something bigger, for something greater? We cannot believe, finally, that we were just made to die. We have a sense of destiny, a sense of bigness, a sense of glory. We cannot get rid of it; we cannot get away from it. Some would have us believe that it can be explained in terms of a great evolutionary impulse that is in us all, urging us on to perfection. But that really does not explain it because what we are all conscious of is the sense, a memory, a recollection, of having lost something. We are ever trying to recapture something that we know we once possessed.

Now that is the first point, but let me hurry on to the second, because it follows of necessity and very logically from the first. The second thing we are told about Adam and Eve is that having become aware of this loss, they then tried to deal with it. They sewed fig leaves together and made themselves aprons. They felt that something had to be done, that they could not remain like this. They said in effect, "How can we cover over this thing that we've lost?" So Adam and Eve made an attempt to cover themselves. The latter part of the chapter tells us how utterly inadequate that was and how God made provision for them. But the point at the moment is that they themselves immediately tried to deal with their loss.

What a wonderful chapter Genesis 3 is! Do you not begin to see how essential it is to a true understanding of life? Has it ever occurred to you that in that one phrase you have a complete summation of the whole history of civilization? What have men and women been doing in this supposed civilization? They have simply been sewing together fig leaves to hide their own nakedness—that is precisely the meaning of what we call "civilization."

Consider some of the ways in which people have tried to do this. First, they are always trying along cultural lines. They say, "What we've lost, of course, is knowledge. There must be some understanding somewhere. Life is an enigma. Life is a problem. Things seem to be contradictory. Human beings themselves are contradictory. We must get out of this." So men and women begin to resort to various cultural ideas and especially to knowledge—the thirst for knowledge, the thirst for understanding.

The book of Job describes this search and says that wisdom is more precious than rubies (28:18). So seek wisdom, discover knowledge. You find this in the book of Ecclesiastes too. There we see man "under the sun" (1:3). That is man apart from his relationship to God. And he is seeking understanding in human wisdom. He says in essence, "If only I could understand man, understand myself, the workings of my very being and of my mind, and the cosmos in which I find myself . . ." That is philosophy, and what is philosophy trying to do? It is trying to make up the loss. We feel we ought to know, that if we only tried harder, we would know. We are trying to cover up the nakedness by means of knowledge.

And not only by direct knowledge, not only by pure thought and philosophy. In their study of history, men and women are really trying to do the same thing and to arrive at understanding. In their love of the arts, in their cultivation of music and so on, they have the feeling that somehow they will make themselves complete, that they will become entire again. They have lost something. How can they get it back? Well, these are the things that they hope will bring them covering and lead to their completion. You are familiar with it all. The world is tremendously busy trying to cover up its nakedness, trying to get back again the glory that has been lost.

Another way, of course, has been through politics. Those who view men and women as being essentially economic units, or just social units, follow that particular line. The human race has always believed, and still believes, that by means of legislation things can somehow or other be put right. People say, "All these deficiencies that we're aware of, all these lacks, well, let's get together and organize something." That is political action; that is the philosophy of politics. It is once more the attempt to put together the fig leaves to cover over a nakedness, to make life whole and complete and rounded and so deal with this sense of being deprived of something. We feel we are entitled to a fullness and to a completeness of life, and so we seek it in this way.

But the extraordinary thing is that, having lost this perfect state through disobedience and rebellion against God, men and women even try to make it up by means of religion. All the religions of the world, the so-called great religions, are nothing but repetitions of this ancient action. They are human beings still trying to answer the question and to fill the gap. Let me give you an illustration from contemporary thought, a most interesting illustration.

Take Aldous Huxley, undoubtedly a brilliant man, a brilliant writer and thinker. Many years ago, Huxley was quite convinced that man could solve his problems and could arrive at a state of completion by means of pure thought. He was one of the leaders of the school that taught that man only has to think and to educate himself and to work things out logically. If he only becomes scientific, said Huxley in his various books and novels, if he only lives a scientific kind of life, then all the problems will be banished and solved, and all will be well.

But Aldous Huxley no longer says that. He came to see that was not the answer. What is it now? Well, now he says that the only thing that can save the world is mysticism, and he has become a Buddhist. In other words, he is aware of the fact that man is not just pure intellect—man has a spirit and feelings and emotions, man is a bigger total than he had thought, and man is crying out for the unseen. There is another realm, Huxley says, another dimension, and he calls it mysticism. He means there is a spiritual realm that is influencing us. And we can only be truly happy and make up our loss as long as we are in accord with that and as long as we submit to that. So now Huxley follows the mystic route, the mystic way. He has turned to religion.

Men and women have been doing this throughout the centuries. Having turned from the only true and living God, they have had to make gods for themselves. They have made their religions. They have tried everything but the God from whom they have departed. And the whole time they repeat this procedure of stitching together a few fig leaves in order to try to hide their nakedness. But it is all inadequate. It is all even ridiculous. It is amateurish. Is it not foolish? Is it not almost laughable?

And yet, you see, that is the very thing that men and women still refuse to recognize. They still scoff at Christianity, and they give themselves to these other things that so often throughout the centuries have been proved to be fatuous. They are trying to cover their nakedness. They are trying somehow or other, by their own efforts, to make up the deficiency, the sense of something lost, something that they still need and cannot find.

And that brings me to the third point, which comes out so prominently in this record. Man has a sense of guilt and a sense of fear. "Adam and his wife hid themselves from the presence of the LORD God amongst the trees of the garden" (Genesis 3:8). You remember that formerly they had accepted the statement of the Devil, "Ye shall not surely die." "There's no need to be afraid," he had said. "Just use your mind and assert yourself and stand up for yourself and express yourself—there's absolutely nothing to fear at all." But Adam and Eve heard the voice of God, and they ran and hid themselves. Why? Because of a sense of fear, a sense of guilt, a sense of shame.

Again, the Bible tells us that is true of all of us. I know we do not like that statement, but we cannot get away from it. It is the simple truth. We like to say that we are masters of our fate and captains of our souls, that we are no longer going to be governed by these phobias and fears, that we take a thoroughly rational, scientific view of life, and that we do what we want to do and what we believe in doing, and we are not going to be frightened by anything. That is all very well in theory and on paper, but alas, like Adam and Eve before us, we find that it is one thing to say but a very different thing to experience. And the whole tragedy of the human race today is that it is in this contradictory position. We say we are not afraid, and yet we are terrified. We say we do not believe in sin and in God, but we have a sense of condemnation. We have a voice within us that accuses us and condemns us. We are filled with a sense of shame. We are unhappy.

You have perhaps said to yourself about a particular action, "There's nothing wrong in that." A temptation came, and you said, "It's all right. I'm no longer living in the mid-Victorian era. I'm not going to be frightened by the shibboleths of religion. I'm not going to be alarmed. I'm taking a scientific view. I have these qualities and powers within me, and they're meant to be exercised. I will exercise them, and all's well." And you did, but you woke up the next morning feeling ashamed, with a sense of condemnation, and it's been gnawing at your conscience ever since. You may have even gone to church for that very reason. You are unhappy, wretched.

There is always a reaction. The stolen fruit is not as pleasant as we had thought. A kind of spiritual indigestion follows the eating of it. Somehow we cannot get away with it. If we could, of course, we would not need any psychologists. But they are doing a thriving business because, though we think we are so bold and so wonderful, something within us tells us that we are cads, that we are cowards, that we are fools, that we are foul, that we are vile, that we are beasts and worse. And we cannot get rid of such a conviction. We cannot sleep because of it. We cannot silence this voice that is within us. If we could we would, but we cannot, and we are wretched, and we have complexes—we will call them that, but we will not call them sin. We will not admit the fear, the shame, the strain, the pressure. Is that not the simple truth? We would like to explain it all away psychologically, but we cannot. We are up against the facts, the facts within ourselves and with respect to ourselves. Though we want to get rid of God and all that belongs to him, we cannot, for the fact is that every man and woman born into this world has a sense of God and a sense of judgment.

Say, if you like, that you do not believe in God, you nevertheless have a sense of God, and you have to argue with yourself. And all your intellectual arguments are really brought forward to boost your own assertion. While you are asserting that you do not believe and that you can prove scientifically that there is no God, something within you is pronouncing against your disbelief and assuring you that there is a God. You are speaking with eloquence in order to drown the voice within you that speaks for God. This is in us all. There is a universal sense of God. Even the most primitive tribes and races have a sense of God and a sense of judgment.

Yes, and coupled with that—I am being brutally frank, am I not?—there is our fear of death.

"Ah," you say, "but modern people aren't afraid of death."

Are they not? Then why do they take so much trouble to avoid speaking about it? Why do they regard it as morbid to be reminded of it? The fact of the matter is that this present age has a horror of death. It is controlled, in a sense, by the fear of death. The Scripture says we are those "who through fear of death were all their lifetime subject to bondage" (Hebrews 2:15).

Let me give you the great statement of that very fact by William Shakespeare. He put the dilemma once and for ever in the words of Hamlet:

> To be, or not to be: that is the question:
> Whether 'tis nobler in the mind to suffer
> The slings and arrows of outrageous fortune,
> Or to take up arms against a sea of troubles.

Here is the problem confronting us all. Is it worth going on with life with all its contradictions and problems, its pains and difficulties, its disappointments and sorrows? Why go on?

A brilliant young Parliament member not many years ago faced up to all this, and he wrote an account of it before he committed suicide. He had a brilliant future before him, and he knew that he had very good prospects of perhaps even becoming Prime Minister. But he worked it out like this: "I know perfectly well that if I go on living and keep my eye on that I shall make many enemies. I do not want to make enemies of them. But because I succeed they will be jealous of me and they will dislike me and they will become my enemies and there will be disappointments, all sorts of things." He asked, "Is it worth it?" And he decided that it was not.

And yet that man was an exceptional person. The average person, as Shakespeare reminds us, does not do that. In the end of Hamlet's soliloquy, he says that he could end it all with a "bare bodkin." He could do it in a second. Well, why not, then? Because, he says:

> . . . who would these fardels [burdens] bear,
> To grunt and sweat under a weary life,
> But that the dread of something after death,
> The undiscover'd country from whose bourn
> No traveler returns, puzzles the will,
> And makes us rather bear those ills we have
> Than fly to others that we know not of?
> Thus conscience doth make cowards of us all,
> And thus the native hue of resolution
> Is sicklied o'er with the pale cast of thought.
>
> *Hamlet*, Act 3, Scene 1

Is that not absolutely true? However intellectual we are, however rational, however calm and cool and collected, we cannot avoid this sense of God, this sense of guilt, this sense of shame, this sense of judgment, this sense of death and what lies beyond it.

> *Dust thou art, to dust returnest,*
> *Was not spoken of the soul.*
>
> Henry Wadsworth Longfellow, "A Psalm of Life"

If these words had been spoken of the soul, very well, I will take up the dagger and end it. But they were not. The soul goes on. And that, as Shakespeare reminds us, cripples the will, as it were. So we decide to go on with life, but the fear remains, and we cannot get away from it. And the guilt and the shame and all the agony and all the remorse and all the kicking of ourselves metaphorically go on and on and on. It started at the beginning, and it has been continuing ever since.

But, lastly, it is here that we see the unutterable folly of man in sin. In his trouble and in his misery and wretchedness, he runs away and hides from God: "Adam and his wife hid themselves from the presence of the LORD God amongst the trees of the garden."

And this is the saddest and most tragic thing of all about man. He runs away from God. In his shame and misery and wretchedness he runs away from the call of God, from the voice of God who comes to him in the garden in the cool of the day.

Why? Well, because he does not know God, because he has believed a lie about him, because he is altogether wrong with respect to him, because he does not realize that the very God against whom he has rebelled and into whose face he has spat is the only one who can save him and that he is prepared to do so. That is the tragedy. There man is, in shame and in failure and in utter hopelessness. And God comes, but man runs and hides. He runs away from God, his only benefactor, his only Savior.

That is the tragedy of the world. Men and women in their misery, in their sin, try everything except what God says to them. I have been making the same point from the very beginning, have I not? We start with the voice from God, the word from God. Man was made in God's image, and he spoke to God, and God spoke to him. But then man listened to the other voice, and he ceased to listen to God, and all his troubles followed. But God speaks again, and again man does not listen. He runs away in fear. And that is precisely what is happening today.

What am I doing as a preacher? I am nothing, and what a privilege is mine. I am just a mouthpiece for God. My dear friend, you who are in sin are being addressed by the voice of God. It is coming to you in the cool of the evening. Are you afraid? Are you resisting him? Are you in some shape or form running away from him? Do you feel that he is against you? Are you rebelling against his message? Are you trying to argue against it and to push it off? Are you afraid of the consequences of listening? If so, you are just repeating what Adam and Eve did. For God came into the garden to tell them that in spite of everything they had done, though he had to punish them for their rebellion, he was also providing a way of salvation and of deliverance. That was exactly why he came. Not merely to denounce them and to pass judgment upon them, but to bring the promise of the seed of the woman and the conquest over the enemy who had misled and defeated them.

That is the message of the gospel, and that is my simple message to you. There is nothing and no one under heaven today able to meet your need except Jesus Christ and him crucified. You are aware of the restlessness, the thirst, the hunger, the searching for something you cannot find. What are you searching for? What do you really need? Let Augustine answer in his great words: "Thou hast made us for thyself, and our souls are restless until they find their rest in thee."

My dear friend, you are made on that scale. Nobody else can satisfy you, no one less than the almighty, eternal God himself. And he does so in Jesus Christ. He brings you back to himself. He will deal with all these subsidiary problems that I have been mentioning. Give up trying to solve them. Give up trying to deliver yourself. Give up trying to get rid of your sense of guilt, for you never will. Your conscience will follow you. As long as you are alive, it will go with you, even beyond the grave, and it will torment you in hell through all eternity. You will never silence it. You will never get rid of a sense of failure, you will never get rid of a sense of guilt and of shame, until you come to Jesus Christ and believe what he tells you—that he has taken your guilt upon himself, that he died for your sins, that

God has punished them on the cross and offers you free pardon. Jesus Christ was crucified on Calvary's hill for that reason and for that reason alone.

And because of that, if you believe in him, the wrath of God no longer abides on you. God assures you that he has pardoned you freely, that he has washed away your sin. He will take away the sense of guilt and of shame. You will know that you are forgiven. You will know that you are a child of God. He will give you new strength and power. He will give you a new understanding. He will give you a new insight. You will see things differently. You will reason differently. You will have a new view of life altogether, a new view of death, a new view of judgment, a new view of eternity, a new view of God himself. Instead of running away from him and whimpering and hiding yourself and feeling that he is against you, you will long, believe me, beyond anything else in this life, to hear the voice of God. You will begin to say:

Speak, I pray thee, gentle Jesus,
Oh, how passing sweet thy words,
Breathing o'er my troubled spirit
Peace which never earth affords.

All the world's distracting voices,
All its enticing tones of ill,
At thine accents, mild, melodious,
Are subdued, and all is still.

William Williams,
"Speak, I Pray Thee, Gentle Jesus"; Edward Griffiths, translator

My beloved friend, have you heard the voice of God speaking to you? He *has* been speaking to you, showing you your failure, your misery, your unhappiness, your wretchedness, the cause of it, how nothing else can ever deliver you out of it, but that he has provided a way in his only begotten Son who gave his life for you because he loved you. Come out of your hiding place. Come to him. Rush to him. Cast yourself at his feet. Say, "I believe."

Just as I am....
With many a conflict, many a doubt.

I don't understand, but nothing else can save me, so—
O Lamb of God, I come, I come.

Charlotte Elliott, "Just as I Am"

And if you do, he will smile upon you and let you know that he has received you. And he will bless you throughout the remainder of your earthly life and in death, and then he will receive you unto himself in glory.

4

"WHERE ART THOU?"

And the LORD God called unto Adam, and said unto him, Where art thou?

GENESIS 3:9

B efore we can possibly understand the meaning of that statement in verse 9, we must look again at the great context. Genesis 3, let me remind you, is one of the most important chapters in the whole Bible because here we have a history of the world and at the same time all the main outlines of salvation. This one chapter summarizes it all for us.

There is a pathetic and ridiculous attitude on the part of so many—an attitude based on nothing but sheer ignorance—that somehow or other the Bible, while a very interesting old book, has nothing to do with the modern world. But it is the very essence of preaching to deal with modern life because the Bible really is concerned about that. It is a timeless book because it is a book about life, a book about the soul. It is a book from God, giving us a view of ourselves and of all others, revealing the causes of our troubles and showing us the sheer waste of energy, apart from anything else, that is involved in trying to solve our problems in any other way except that which is offered to us so freely in our Lord and Savior Jesus Christ.

So here is the history without which we cannot understand why the whole world, and each one of us in particular, is as it is at this moment. There is no other explanation. Many other answers are

THE GOSPEL IN GENESIS
THE GOSPEL IN GENESIS

being offered, of course, and we are familiar with them. But our position is that having looked at them all, and having perhaps tried many of them and having found them all to fail—as the Bible tells us from the beginning that they must and will—we come back to this. The biblical message authenticates itself in experience. It has done so throughout the centuries, and its claim is that it is as true today as it has ever been and is as relevant to men and women in their predicament today as it was a thousand or two thousand or even three thousand years ago.

Now that is the general position. And I have been anxious to emphasize that this chapter is not only a record of actual history but in addition is a full explanation of what each one of us does in our lives. That is the remarkable thing about the Bible. That is why it gives us so much history. Each of us in our turn repeats what was done at the beginning, and we go on repeating it. That is why there is, as the author of Ecclesiastes tells us, "no new thing under the sun" (1:9). And there really is not as far as men and women are concerned.

If you think that we are all so different today, just make a list of the things that people are doing in London or wherever at this moment—you will find that these were all being done in Old Testament times. Not in exactly the same form perhaps, but still the same things. There is no difference. You will find it all here. For all their cleverness and brilliant advances and inventions, men and women seem to be quite incapable of inventing a new sin. Have you ever thought of that? The sins we commit have all been thought of before, and they have all been practiced. According to the Bible— and I suggest to you that our own experiences and the history of the world to this moment confirm this teaching—man as a being does not change at all. So what we find in the third chapter of Genesis is true today of every human individual in this world.

We have seen that there is one real cause of all our troubles, and that is our wrong attitude toward God—everything stems from that. So we have been spending our time, in particular, tracing and analyzing that wrong attitude. We considered it first from the aspect of the intellect, and then we went on to think about some of the consequences—the persistent sense of loss and incompleteness, the guilt and shame, the fear of life and the fear of death. Finally, we have seen how even when God comes to us, we run away from him because of our totally wrong idea concerning him. Our final tragedy is that we refuse the one thing that can put us right.

Now we go on from there because the story goes on. We have seen what man did that produced the Fall, and we have seen what he is like as a result of the Fall. So you might have thought that the story would end there. But it does not. It goes on, and it must go on. And that is a central message of the Bible.

Why does the story go on? Well, according to this record, it is because, whether we like it or not, this is God's world. And you cannot stop God from coming to his world, his own property, his own possession. We never like that, of course. That is the whole essence of our modern objection to God, the objection of people as they are by nature. We think we have got rid of him and have finished with him. We are now going to carry on without God. And we constantly decide to do that. But remember the eighth verse of Genesis 3: "And they heard the voice of the LORD God walking in the garden in the cool of the day: and Adam and his wife hid themselves from the presence of the LORD God amongst the trees of the garden," as if to say, "If we only get behind there and hide, he'll just walk straight on, and then we'll be able to come out again, and all will be well. And if we hear him again, we'll go hide again."

But the backs of the trees belong to God quite as much as the fronts of the trees. The whole garden belongs to God. The universe is God's. So the story has to go on. And this is the first principle, surely, that we all need to learn and to grasp. We are not independent creatures in this world. We do not own it, and we cannot order it and decide what happens in it. That is the first great lesson here. It is God from beginning to end. It is God making his world. He owns it. It is his possession. He controls it. He sustains it. He guides it. He interferes with it. He comes into it. He erupts into it. It is always God's. That is the lesson—God coming into the garden when Adam and Eve thought that they had finished with him.

And what God does, as we are reminded here, is this: he continues to speak. That is the thing. We see this here from beginning to end. God made man in his own image, and he spoke to him. And man listened and replied. That was perfection. That was paradise. That was man as he was meant to be. God speaking—man listening to God. The greatest thing man can ever know is to be spoken to by God. But man decided to stop that. He did not want that anymore. He did not believe in that any longer. And he thought it ended there. But God went on speaking.

Adam and Eve hid at the back of the trees, but this is what happened: "And the LORD God called unto Adam, and said unto him, Where art thou?" (v. 9). And they heard God, and they could not avoid him, and they had to come out of hiding.

"Where art thou?"

It was God speaking. Oh, yes, God speaks to men and women! That is the great message of the Bible. God addresses us in many different ways—he speaks in the conscience, he speaks in history, he speaks in events. You cannot understand history apart from that. We find a great deal of this, and certainly the only adequate explanation of it, in God's book. Even in secular history God speaks in an endless number of ways. But we are all deaf as the result of sin and do not hear him.

God does not always speak with an audible voice as he spoke to Adam and Eve hiding there behind the trees. In the book of Job we are told that sometimes, when man has become impervious, God speaks by dreams and visions in the night (4:13; 7:14). He speaks through accidents, through illnesses, through death. Supremely he speaks in this Word of his, which is his word addressed to us. And then, beyond it all, God speaks to us in his Son: "God, who at sundry times and in divers manners spake in time past unto the fathers by the prophets, hath in these last days spoken unto us by his Son" (Hebrews 1:1–2).

So let us now concentrate on how God speaks, because it is all suggested to us, it seems to me, in this ninth verse of Genesis 3 and in some of the following verses.

The first thing I notice is that God addresses us personally. "And the LORD God called unto Adam, and said unto him, Where art thou?" "Where art *thou?*" It was a personal address to Adam. Here is one of the truths that we must grasp at the very outset. We all know by experience that there is nothing we are so slow to understand as this fact. Do you see what happened? Before we come to this verse, we find a good deal of conversation by other people, and they have been talking about God. "Yea," said the Devil, "hath God said . . . ?" And Eve replied, "Yes, God has said . . ." Adam and Eve and the Devil were, as it were, having a conversation about God, and they were expressing their opinions about him. But suddenly, in this ninth verse, the whole situation changed. Now God was addressing Adam and Eve as they were hiding behind the trees. The positions were reversed. And that is the first thing that happens to a man or woman who is on the way to becoming a Christian. The first thing we become conscious of is that we are being addressed. To put it another way, Adam suddenly found that far from being the investigator, he was the one being investigated.

"Adam, where art thou?"

The Lord God had come down, and he was looking. He was searching. Adam and his position and condition were under investigation. Before that, Adam had been walking around the garden. He had listened to the Devil's suggestion and had thought he was in a position of supremacy. He was looking on, and he was expressing his opinions. But now he found himself being addressed, under examination, investigated.

Surely my meaning is perfectly clear. If you have a discussion with people about religion and about Christianity, you will always find that they talk as the investigators. Ha! With their great brains they are going to look into this question of the Bible. They are going to investigate God. They have the ability. And God? Well, God is a kind of specimen, as it were, to be put on the table, to be dissected, to be analyzed, to be considered. Modern man is investigating the universe, investigating religion, investigating God. Man is on the throne; he is the judge on the bench. Ah, yes, he has considered Buddhism and Confucianism and Hinduism. Now he will try Christianity. "Well now, what about Christ . . . ?"

I am not caricaturing this, am I? Have we not all done this? We imagine that we are in a position to investigate. But suddenly we are brought to the realization that we are the ones who are being examined, that we have been betraying ourselves without realizing it. And the more we talk, the more we betray ourselves and the more we are examined.

I want to ask a question. Have you realized, my friend, that in this life you are on trial? You are not doing the trying. You are being tried. Shall I sum this up by putting it in terms of what a great man once said? Referring to a man who had remarked that he saw absolutely nothing in the novels of Sir Walter Scott, this great man commented that such a person was not telling us anything about Scott but was telling us a very great deal about himself! How true that is. And it is exactly the same with regard to this whole matter of investigating God. We fondly imagine that we are in the position of examiners, but suddenly something happens to us, and we are conscious of the fact that we are being looked at, that we are being addressed, that we are being spoken to, that a word has come to us.

Have you reached that stage, my friend? Have you realized that in this world we are workers and travelers and are not simply spectators sitting in a gallery looking on at some game that is being played by other people in the arena? Do you not realize that you are involved and that every second you live, judgments are being formed about you and that by what you do here you are determining not only what happens to you in this world but also in eternity?

But let me put that in a slightly different form. Adam was suddenly made to realize that he was not only being addressed but that it was he himself as a person who was being considered. What was under investigation was not merely his ideas and his thoughts and his position in a philosophical sense but he himself. And this is absolutely true about us all. Christianity is not a matter of opinions. When God addresses us in the various ways that I have indicated, he is not talking to us about our opinions. He is not a bit interested in them. He is interested in us. "Where art thou? I am speaking to you. Adam, where are *you*?" That is what God says.

But how cleverly we avoid all this. We are ready to express our opinions and to have our arguments. We think that Christianity is a matter for discussion. What do you start with? Well, you may start, if you like, with the being of God. Then, having dealt with that, we say, "Of course, there's this question of miracles. Are miracles possible? Can they happen?" So we may spend another evening discussing miracles. This is all *discussing* Christianity, is it not? We think that is what Christianity is about.

And then we come to Jesus of Nazareth and the Christian claim that he was God and man, that there were two natures in that one Person. Well, we must spend at least a night on this. Let's have this out. Is that possible? Is it conceivable?

Then there is this question of Jesus' death on a cross on Calvary's hill, the great doctrine about something called "atonement"—that one died for others, that he made himself a substitute, and so on. So we take this up. Is this even moral? Is it conceivable? Can it happen? We spend a whole night arguing about that.

And the whole time we think we have been discussing Christianity. There is a sense, of course, in which we have, but there is another sense in which we have not, because, my friend, you can not only go to your grave but you can even go to hell just doing that. Christianity, primarily, is not a discussion about ideas. It is a discussion about *you*.

"Adam, where art thou? I am looking for you. I am interested in you, the individual person."

And that is the first thing men and women realize when they are on their way to becoming Christians. Throughout their lives they have never faced themselves at all. They have been protecting themselves. They have been putting up camouflage to conceal themselves. That is the meaning of all the arguments and disputations about these various questions. "Something is coming that's going to be a little bit personal and may be difficult. Very well, let's hide behind the trees." And we hide behind the trees of these philosophies and ideas and comparative religions and abstruse questions, and as long as we are there, it is all outside us. But God penetrates through it all.

It is about you, my friend, you as an individual at this moment. It is all about you and your life and what you are doing with it and where you are going. Has it come personally to you yet?

May I ask another question? Do you resent this personal emphasis? Lord Melbourne, one of the Victorian prime ministers, spoke for many a modern man when he said, "Things have come to a very pretty pass if religion's going to start being personal."

"Adam, where art thou?"

Have you realized that this is a personal matter? A personal decision? A personal coming face-to-face with God? You are confronted by God. God is addressing you. God is speaking to you—to *you*! He is not interested primarily in your ideas but in you yourself as you pass through this life and through this world once and once only.

What next? Well, the next step is that God forces us to face where we are and what we are. "Adam, *where* art thou? Where exactly are you, and what are you doing there?" In other words, this whole business of preaching and of the gospel brings me face-to-face with the fact of where I am and of where I ought to be. Before, when God, as it were, came into that garden called paradise, Adam was always there to meet him. He looked forward to his coming, rejoiced in his coming, ran to meet him with a smile on his face. But now, for the first time, he did not do that; he was hiding behind some trees. And God said, "Where are you? You have never been there before. What are you doing there? Come out. That is not the place for you. You ought not to be there; you ought to be here."

And that is precisely what God is asking every one of us at this moment. "Where are you? Where are you in life and in this world?" Let me subdivide this. Where are you intellectually? Where are you in your thinking? Have you really faced all the facts? May I put it as simply and as bluntly and as plainly as this? You may say to me that you have long since rejected Christianity. Well, I only want to ask one question: have you ever read the Bible through? I have found that all of us tend to dismiss Christianity without really knowing what it is. We have never really taken the trouble to find out. We have dismissed it as a prejudice. We have not read the Bible, we have not even read the New Testament, we know nothing about the history of the church—yet we dismiss it all.

I say that is intellectually dishonest. Where are we, I repeat, in the matter of the mind and the whole process of thought and the complete view of life? Have we really brought in all the factors? Have we included life itself in our conduct and our behavior? Have we listened to the voice of conscience? Have we looked into the face of death? Have we looked beyond? Have we considered the testimony of some of the best and the greatest people that the world has ever known? Have we read the history of revivals? Where are we intellectually? Have we really brought all this in?

That is the challenge of the Word of God. God knows perfectly well that we hide behind these intellectual trees. I have already mentioned a number of them. But as long as you are there, you are not seeing things clearly. You must come out into the open, says the Bible, and really face the truth.

"Ah," you say, "but I've always thought that Christianity is sob stuff."

That is because you have dismissed it without considering it. Christianity is reasonable. It is valid argument. It has a case. It comes to you as a fully-orbed revelation of the truth of God. You will find this discussed in many books. For example, you cannot dispute the brainpower of C. S. Lewis, can you? Read his book *Surprised by Joy*, in which he tells you something of his history in these matters. But he is only one of many. My friends, it is intellectually dishonest to say that Christianity is not intellectually respectable. That is hiding behind trees. That is a refusal to come out into the open and really face it all and really try it. So I say that the Bible asks where we are intellectually.

In the same way, and perhaps with much more insistence, the Bible comes to us and asks us where we are morally. Oh, how much easier it is to argue about philosophy and theology than to face ourselves in a moral sense. Where are we in the matter of chastity? In the matter of purity? In the matter of honesty? In the matter of soul cleanliness? In the whole matter of our life and living? That is the first thing, surely, that we all ought to be considering. Before you try to understand miracles, let me commend to you that you start trying to understand yourself.

Why do we go on doing things that we know to be wrong? Why do we get pleasure from that? Why do we continue, though we know that we will have pain later on? Why do we do such things? That is the problem. That is the real issue facing men and women— not their grand opinions about abstractions, but they themselves.

"Adam, where are you?"

Where are you morally? What of the credit, the moral credit, with which you began? What is the account like at this moment? What if the books were opened in public? What if your life and your story could be flashed onto a screen? That is what the Bible is interested in. That is what it is talking about. It is personal, and it is direct, and it is about our own lives.

Let me give you the supreme example of this. It is to be found in the Scriptures, in the fourth chapter of the Gospel according to John, where we read of our Lord's dealings with a woman of Samaria. Our Lord was tired, so he sat down by the side of the well, and the woman came along to draw water. At once they began to converse. They talked about Jews and Samaritans, and they talked about the well and the depth of the well and about Jacob who had dug the well. And the woman was enjoying the conversation and was arguing very cleverly. They talked about God and about worship.

But in the middle of all this, our Lord suddenly said, "Go, call thy husband, and come hither." The woman had to reply honestly and say, "I have no husband." And our Lord looked at her and said, "Thou hast well said, I have no husband: For thou hast had five husbands; and he whom thou now hast is not thy husband: in that saidst thou truly" (John 4:16–18).

That is the Lord Jesus Christ's method. He puts an end to all the argument and disputation about a thousand and one questions. He brings it right home to the woman herself. Here is a woman who would talk about God and about worship, and yet she was living in adultery, and our Lord made her face it. "Come out," he said in essence, "from behind that tree. Come out into the open. I know all about you."

"Adam, *where* art thou?"

And that is the thing that God is saying to all of us. My dear friend, face yourself and your own life—what you are actually doing, what you actually are, the thoughts that you fondle, the imaginations that you delight in, the things you do, the things that you know perfectly well are in your mind and you are ashamed of them. You would not publicly confess that you are guilty of them all. That is what God is talking about. That is Christianity. "Adam, come out from that hiding place." Is this clear, my friends?

Let me give you just one other illustration of this, from the Old Testament, the famous story of David. We are told that David was suddenly tempted, and his lust got the better of him. He committed adultery, and then, to cover it over, he committed murder. And he thought all was well, but God had seen it, and God was displeased. So God sent his servant Nathan to talk to David.

Nathan put a conundrum to David. "O king," he said, "something has happened." And he painted a picture of a man who, though he had many sheep, stole the only sheep belonging to another man. Hearing this, David was filled with wrath and indignation and said that man had to be punished. Nothing was too severe for him.

Then Nathan paused, looked at David, and said, "Thou art the man." He said in essence, "I'm speaking about you, David. You thought that I was putting a question of inequity to you and discussing a moral problem in general. But, King David, I have been speaking about *you*" (2 Samuel 12:1–7).

"Adam, where art thou?"

It is you, your life, your moral behavior, your total personality that is under investigation.

The next point that I must emphasize is this: when God comes to us and speaks to us personally, he makes us realize the true nature and character of what we have just been doing. He puts it like this: "Who told thee that thou wast naked? Hast thou eaten of the tree, whereof I commanded thee that thou shouldest not eat?" (Genesis 3:11). God made Adam and Eve face the exact nature of what they had done. It was not just a question of eating fruit. They had broken his commandment, they had violated his holy law, they had raised themselves up in rebellion against him. God brought it right home to them.

And, you know, the gospel does that. It fixes and establishes sin. How does it do that? Well, it teaches the true nature of sin. I have just been discussing the case of David. Let me come back to it again. David, after he had seen the truth and after he had repented, sat down and wrote Psalm 51, and in that psalm, in which he dealt with this very sin that he had committed, he put it like this: "Against thee, thee only, have I sinned, and done this evil in thy sight" (v. 4). David meant that the terrible thing about his sin, the thing that makes sin sin, was not so much that he had been guilty of adultery and of murder, though that was bad enough, but that he had sinned against God. He had violated the law of God. He was a rebel against God. That is the reality that we do not see. We are prepared, perhaps, to admit the category of sin, of wrongdoing, but we regard it as merely some transgression of a moral code, the breaking of a law, and we say there is no more to it than that. But, my dear friend, there is.

You and I, as human beings, were made in the image of God. And we were meant to live a life that such persons should live. We were meant to be in correspondence with God and to live in enjoyment of him. We were meant to be righteous and holy and true and upright. And what is sin? It is a departure from that. The trouble, is it not, is that we all tend to think of sin only in terms of particular actions. But the terrible thing about sin is that it is a violation of God's creation. It is robbery of God. It is spitting into the face of God. Any life today that is not lived to the glory of God is in the depth of sin. God made Adam see all this, and Eve saw it, and anyone who comes under conviction of sin must of necessity see it.

So the final question for all of us is just this: where are you at this moment? Do you know God? Do you love him? Do you delight in him? Is it your greatest concern to please him and to live to his glory and to his honor? God would have you see that unless that is your purpose, you are a vile sinner. He brings that home to you. You have departed from where he put you. You are hiding somewhere. You are out of the pathway. You are somewhere where you should not be. And you are transgressing the law of God and who you were meant to be. God brings us to see that.

Is that not what is so lacking in the modern world? Many people believe in respectability, but they do not believe in God. And they are terrible sinners—as terrible as the people who are living in the gutters of London at this moment. Sin is against God. "I have sinned," says the prodigal son to his father. "I have sinned against heaven, and in thy sight" (Luke 15:21). That is the nature of sin, and it is always true of us.

But that brings me to my last point, which is that God, when he thus comes to us and speaks to us, not only gives us a personal address, but in order to bring us to repentance, he then proceeds to tell us about judgment. You remember how he did it there in the garden at the beginning. God came to Adam and Eve and, having drawn them out of their hiding place and having shown them themselves and their sin, he pronounced judgment.

I am sorry, my friend, if you do not like the idea of judgment. No natural person has ever liked judgment. But whether we like it or not, it is a fact. God himself revealed his judgment at the very beginning. He came after man. You cannot get away from God. Of course, you can walk away from church and say you will never come back again, but that is not walking out of God's universe, that is not walking out of God's sight. You can hide yourself, get away, rush into the thickets and imagine that he will not see you. But he will call you out just as he has always called man out of hiding. God's judgment is being repeated in the history of the world and of every human individual at this very moment.

And what is God's judgment? Well, you can subdivide it into the present and the future. There is an immediate judgment that always comes as a result of sin. What is that? Well, God pronounced in Genesis 3 that there would be a perpetual conflict between the serpent and the woman and between the seed of the serpent and the seed of the woman. And is that not absolutely true? Are we not all in this conflict, and do we not know all about it? Consider temptation—evil drawing us, enticing us, battling against that which is best and noblest and most upright in us. Do you not see this everywhere—in the newspapers, on the billboards, in all places of amusement, on the streets? This struggle between the seed of the serpent and the seed of the woman is the whole problem of life and of existence. The moment we enter into this life we are already in the fight. The battle of morality. The battle of purity. The battle of chastity. The battle of honesty. And what a fight it is! The current is dragging us down. How difficult it is to fight against it and to battle upstream. This is a verification of God's judgment.

But the blindness that sin produces in us prevents us from seeing that all this is nothing but part of God's judgment on sin. Man thought that by listening to the Devil and eating that forbidden fruit

he was going to have an easy time, that there would be an end of
conformity to law, that he would be a god, that he would be absolutely free. But he put himself into shackles and into chains, and he
has been struggling in them ever since. The seed of the serpent and
the seed of the woman are locked in this endless fight between the
hell that life can be and God's plan for us. We have all known it,
and not only that, but the sorrow and the suffering too. "In sorrow
thou shalt bring forth children" (Genesis 3:16), in pain and suffering. This is history. These are facts.

That, my friend, is part of God's judgment. It is all part of God's
pronouncement on rebellion and sin. What greater joy is there than
the coming of a child into a family? But think of the accompanying strain, the struggle, the suffering, the oft-repeated sorrow. It is
sin that produces all that. It is the wrong attitude toward God. It is
man's rebellion against God. It is man taking the law unto himself.
That is why there is all this suffering and sorrow and illness and
disease and pain and all the problems.

But not only that, there is the very struggle for existence—the
toil of earning one's livelihood, getting one's daily bread, the hard-
ness, the thorns and the thistles, the competition and the troubles.
Why is it that thorns and thistles grow so abundantly? Why is it so
difficult to get a crop of wheat or corn out of the ground? Why this
endless fighting, with everything against us? All we get we have to
work for with the very sweat of our brow. Again, this is just part
of God's judgment on sin. And men and women have been trying
to deal with it and to cope with it ever since, but they cannot. They
would like to get back to that paradise, but they have been driven
out. God drove Adam and Eve out, and he put at the entrance the
cherubim and the flaming sword turning in every direction. And
though man in civilization has been rushing against that gate and
trying to burst through, the flaming sword keeps him back. The
whole story of civilization, in a sense, is a story of futility, a history
of failure.

Even some great historians who are not Christians at all talk of the cyclical theory of history. We ever seem to be advancing. We are on the point of getting there. But we just go around the other side of the circle, and we are back where we were. Civilization goes round and round in cycles. There is no forward advance. There is no end. There is no reaching the ultimate objective. Life is simply a futile procedure. Round and round we go. We rise. We succeed. We fail. We fall. Down they go—dynasties, empires, individuals. That is always true. It is because of the flaming sword and the cherubim at the east end of the garden of Eden. Man will never get back there by his own efforts; he is incapable of it. He is not allowed to; he has been driven out—that is the judgment upon sin. But that is only the present; there is something beyond.

"And unto dust shalt thou return" (Genesis 3:19). Death, physical death, came in as part of the punishment of sin. Tennyson tells us:

> [Man] thinks he was not made to die.
>
> "In Memoriam"

That is just part of man's recollection of what he once was. But as he is now, he has the seeds of mortality within him. The moment he is born, he is beginning to die. A little baby was born a second ago. You say that there at any rate is someone who is beginning to live. I can say with equal accuracy that there is someone who has started dying. The first breath is but the first of a series that is leading to the last. That is not being morbid; that is being factual. We are born to die. Death, the inevitable end, comes to pass, and beyond it we face God.

My dear friends, you know you have to face all that. And you do not come to the garden until you have. This is no sob story. This is not a patent remedy. This is not one of your optimistic philosophies. This is not a kind of spiritual outlook that says, "Come along, let's be bright and cheerful and happy and walk with a new step; it's all right." It is terribly wrong. And God would have us see how terribly wrong it is.

Do you realize where you are? Where are you at this moment? How long have you lived in this world? How much longer do you think you are going to be here? What have you done with your life? What have you made of it? What is your record? Are you proud of it? What are your achievements? What is your secret life? What is the history of your mind and your thought and your imagination and your heart?

"Adam, where are you?"

In every respect, where are you, man? Where are you, woman? Come out of that hiding place and face the truth, for you have to. You are in God's world. You are God's creature, and you cannot avoid him. You cannot evade him. You have to deal with him. And if you do not listen to him in life, you will have to listen to him in death. When your name is called out at the great judgment throne in eternity, you will have to step forward and listen to the verdict.

But I must not stop there. I know that nobody will really listen to what I am about to say who does not believe what I have just been saying. It is only the desperate who come to Christ. It is only those who know they are sick who see their need of the physician. But thank God there is the physician.

I told you about the judgment, but God went on. There is to be this struggle between the seed of the serpent and the seed of the woman, but the seed of the woman shall bruise the serpent's head (Genesis 3:15). The God who calls you to come out of your hiding place calls you out not only to condemn you but to tell you that he has made a way to bring you back to paradise, if you believe and acknowledge the condemnation. He tells you that he has sent his only Son, the seed of the woman, into this world to do something that when he advances makes the cherubim and the flaming sword fall back and allow us in. Jesus of Nazareth, the Son of God, has borne the judgment of the sin of all who believe in him and who look to him. And if you trust in him, he will take you through the gate into the joy of the Lord. And if you enter in with him now, you will be able to say:

Today thy mercy calls us to wash away our sin;
However great our trespass, whatever we have been;
However long from mercy we may have turned away,
Thy blood, O Christ, can cleanse us, and make us white today.

Thank God for this gospel because:

When all things seem against us, to drive us to despair,
We know one gate is open, one ear will hear our prayer.

Oswald Allen[5]

If you have heard God speaking to you, cry out to him for mercy, and he will not refuse you. "Him that cometh to me I will in no wise cast out" (John 6:37). So from your hiding place of failure and shame and misery and unhappiness, come out and cry to him, and he will deliver you.

5

TRUE HISTORY

And I will put enmity between thee and the woman, and between thy seed and her seed; it shall bruise thy head, and thou shalt bruise his heel.

GENESIS 3:15

We have been considering the all-important message of Genesis 3, and we have been doing so because, it seems to me, it is good from time to time deliberately to stand back and take a large and comprehensive view of the message of the Bible. Many today seem to think that the Bible is irrelevant and remote from life and that it does not meet us where we are, in the midst of our problems and our difficulties. So I have been at pains to show that the exact opposite is the truth. No book in the world today comes to us in the particular way that the Bible comes to us, exactly where we are, in our exact predicament. In other words, this third chapter of the book of Genesis is absolutely essential to a true understanding of life, the whole of life as it is at this moment for each individual.

We are all confronted by many problems. We all have our own personal needs. No one is perfectly happy. Things go wrong. We all know what it is to be miserable. We all know what it is to have a sense of failure. We are all seeking for something that we do not have. What is the explanation? This is not just a theoretical problem. Why are there wars and tumults and uncertainties and disappointments? What is it all about?

I have been trying to say that there are only two possible

answers to all those questions. We either accept the teaching of this book, the Bible, or we do not. I put all other answers into the second category. They are not the biblical answer, and that is the important thing about them. The Bible is a message about life, about people and their problems and troubles. That is why, in addition to its teaching, it gives us history. It tells us about nations and what happened to them, about individuals and what took place in their lives. It is the most practical book in the world. And it tells us that it comes to us with a message from God about life itself and about our lives in particular.

My suggestion has been that all of that is included in this one chapter in Genesis. Here is the most important key to history that is available at this moment. It explains the past. It explains the present. It explains the future. Let me put it as plainly as this: this is not allegory. I have no gospel unless this is history. In addition, I have been pointing out that as well as being a literal historical record of something that actually happened, Genesis 3 is also, in the most amazing way, an account and a description of the very thing that happens to us one by one. For the astounding fact is that every one of us repeats the action of Adam and Eve.

We have been looking at Adam and Eve's disobedience in different ways. First, we considered it from the standpoint of the intellect, and then we turned to some of the consequences of their action—beginning with the feeling that we have lost something and our attempts to cover ourselves, which always fail. Then we looked at some further consequences. Our theme was man's idea that he could turn his back on God and live an independent life. But we saw that Adam and Eve could not escape from God. God searched them out and addressed them personally. And our point was that God still does that.

We have all been hiding behind these trees—behind the camouflage we put up and the problems that we say confront us. We will argue about anything as long as we can keep the gospel message away from us. No doubt many of us would find it much more interesting and entertaining if I presented a theme from the headlines in the daily newspapers, but I regard that as one of the trees. If I gave my opinion about divorce, for example, you who are not confronted by that particular problem would feel happy about yourself, but your sin would not be dealt with.

One Sunday morning a representative of the Press Association approached me before the service, wanting to know if I was going to consider the theme of many newspapers at that time. My only reply was that I never find my sermons in the headlines of newspapers and that, furthermore, I was going to preach about something of much greater concern to every newspaper reader, but I was certain it would not be printed because it would not be considered sensational.

The most sensational thing in the world at this moment is that every man and woman born into this life is under the wrath of God, and unless they believe in the Lord Jesus Christ, that wrath will abide upon them. The newspapers, though, are not interested in that. We are always interested in somebody else and some other problem remote from us. There are the trees. But the gospel brings us out of hiding, and we must face God alone. "Adam, where art thou?" It is a personal question.

So that is more or less the point at which we have arrived. It all seems hopeless, does it not? Man fell from his first estate. He was driven out of paradise, and the flaming sword made it impossible to get back. Life is full of toil. We are contending with thorns and thistles. Children are brought forth in pain and suffering. Death has come in. The world is in a state of chaos. That is the position in which we find ourselves.

But then God enters the picture! History does not end at that point. That is not the end of the story. And that is why I call myself a minister of the gospel of the Lord Jesus Christ. Into this hopelessness and wretchedness and despair comes a pronouncement and a proclamation. God is revealing to us his plan and his purpose.

And it is to this that I am now anxious to call your attention as it is put to us so perfectly and in such a gloriously succinct manner in the fifteenth verse of the third chapter of the book of Genesis. Here, way back in the garden of Eden, is the first pronouncement and proclamation of the Christian gospel. How utterly ignorant they are who think that because we are Christians we do not need the Old Testament. That shows a complete failure to understand the New Testament gospel. The two must go together, the Old and the New. Why? Because it is the same God operating throughout. And there, back at the beginning, he made this announcement, this proclamation.

So let me try to summarize it by putting it to you like this: What is the message? What is the position confronting us? It is that whether we like it or not, the Devil is controlling this world. That is where the history has brought us—man and his folly. As Eve put it in her reply to God, "The serpent beguiled me" (Genesis 3:13). As Adam and Eve were beguiled in that way, so the whole of humanity has been beguiled, and the result is that men and women have put themselves under the dominion and control of the Devil. Now let us be perfectly clear about this—I am asserting that this is the only way to understand the history of the world. As I said at the beginning, we are concerned about contemporary history, about the state of the human race at this very moment, and about our own personal problems. And the question is, why are things as they are?

There is only one adequate answer. It is the work of the Devil. We are under the control and in the power of the Devil. That is why things are as they are. That is why they have been as they have been. That is the whole explanation of history. Men and women left to themselves are absolutely hopeless and helpless in the hands of the Devil.

Someone may say, "Ah, yes, but you're basing all that on the third chapter of Genesis, and, of course, I no longer accept that. As science now knows, this can't be true. It is just allegory, fantasy."

And, of course, the simple reply is that science has nothing to do with it at all. Science has nothing to do with history. Science is supposed to deal with facts, and when scientists go beyond that, they cease to be scientists and are trying to be philosophers. And then they are simply expressing opinions that are of no more value than the opinions of people who have never had any scientific training at all.

But, my dear friends, my point is that I am not basing my argument solely on the third chapter of Genesis. This is how the Lord Jesus Christ put it:

> When a strong man armed keepeth his palace, his goods are in peace: but when a stronger than he shall come upon him, and overcome him, he taketh from him all his armour wherein he trusted, and divideth his spoils. (Luke 11:21–22)

Our Lord's picture of humanity in sin, humanity as the result of what happened in paradise, is that the whole human race is like a number of people in a great castle. Surrounding the castle there is a mighty wall, built to an enormous height, and the castle is governed by a powerful chieftain. The "strong man armed keepeth his palace, his goods are in peace." In a very subtle way, he allows the people a certain amount of liberty. It is a big castle. There are extensive grounds. There is a sort of parkland, and you can walk around. And some people imagine that because they are not chained in the corner of a cell and can move about, they have absolute liberty. But the fact is that the liberty is only within the confines of the palace. Try to get out if you can! Try to scale those walls! Try to make a breach in them! Make any effort to get into that world that is outside the palace walls and you will find yourself clubbed back in helplessness. "When a strong man armed keepeth his palace, his goods are in peace." They are absolutely under his control. That is the view of men and women in sin that is held by the Son of God himself.

And, of course, the servants of our Lord have repeated what he said. Indeed, the risen Lord himself said it again to one of his most notable servants. When Saul of Tarsus saw the risen Lord on the road to Damascus, the Lord gave him a commission. He said he was sending Paul out as a preacher and as an apostle: "[I am] delivering thee from the people, and from the Gentiles, unto whom now I send thee"—what for?—"to open their eyes, and to turn them from darkness to light, and from the power of Satan unto God" (Acts 26:17–18). There it is again: "from the power of Satan unto God." So it is not surprising that this man, when he became the apostle Paul, in writing to the Galatians, praised God for the Lord Jesus Christ "who gave himself for our sins, that he might deliver us from this present evil world" (Galatians 1:4). And in the epistle to the Colossians Paul says it again: "who hath delivered us from the power of darkness, and hath translated us into the kingdom of his dear Son" (1:13). This teaching is found throughout Scripture.

By nature, then, men and women are under the dominion and the authority and the power of the Devil, who rules this world. He is "the god of this world" (2 Corinthians 4:4). He is "the prince of the power of the air, the spirit that now worketh in the children of disobedience" (Ephesians 2:2). So the problem confronting every man and woman in this world is not just a problem of certain sins and weaknesses, nor the desire to get the happiness that they do not have, together with a certain amount of understanding and hope and joy—those are not their problems. The problem confronting every one of us is how to escape from the dominion of Satan, how to get out of the clutches of the Devil, how, somehow, to make an exit out of the kingdom of darkness into the light and knowledge of God, how to get back into that paradise from which we have been thrust, how to get past that flaming sword. That is the problem.

And the whole tragedy of the world today is that men and women do not realize that. All the systems of philosophy, the educational systems, and the cults know nothing about that, and they are not interested. They are out to make you feel happier. They say, "Of course, we know you're miserable and you'd like to be happy. Very well. Do what we tell you, and we'll make you happy." And up to a point they succeed. But you can be happy on the grounds of the armed strong man. There are poor lunatics who are happy in asylums. There are poor drunkards who, having taken a certain amount of alcohol, feel perfectly happy—everything in the world is fine. They were depressed before they began to drink. That is why they drank. But now the problem is gone; nothing at all is wrong. But, oh, the tragedy is that they are in bondage, more so than ever. The cults and all these other agencies say they can help us in this respect, and they can. But they never face our ultimate problem, the radical difficulty—the dominion of Satan, this position that man got himself into way back in paradise.

I must add, even at the risk of being misunderstood, that any evangelism, so called, that does not deal with this fundamental problem is a false evangelism. The test to apply is not whether we feel happy or better, not whether we have a joy that we did not have before or have shed certain sins, but whether we have come out from under the dominion of Satan. Do we know God? Are we reconciled to him? Are we really in the light? Those are the questions.

And this is all put before us in the Bible. The apostle Paul tells us, in a striking passage in 2 Corinthians:

> But if our gospel be hid, it is hid to them that are lost: in whom the god of this world hath blinded the minds of them which believe not, lest the light of the glorious gospel of Christ, who is the image of God, should shine unto them. (4:3–4)

Satan blinds the mind. The captivity is such that we are not allowed to think straightly. We are not allowed to see the meaning of the gospel.

There is the problem. That is the situation. What can be done? I have already told you that man can do nothing about it. And until you have come to see and to believe and to accept that, you cannot possibly accept the gospel that is to follow. None of us will believe in Christ if we think we can put ourselves right. We have to see our hopelessness as sinners before we can ever see our need of the Savior. Men and women are totally helpless. They are like Adam and Eve, shivering, frightened, alarmed, terrified, not knowing what to do, listening to the pronouncement of judgment, and thrust out into the misery and wretchedness and hopelessness of life.

But, thank God, I repeat that this is not the end of the story. God now announced and revealed his program, in this fifteenth verse of this third chapter of the book of Genesis. I will never allow anybody to take this out of my Bible. It is my gospel. It is the beginning of it all. I do not understand it apart from this. This is the whole message of the Bible. It is a message to the effect that God will conquer and defeat Satan and deliver people from that enemy's foul dominion. It is nothing less than that. That is how God himself announced his own gospel. It is not simply an announcement that he will make us happier and better and brighter. Not at all! The purpose is to deliver us out of that bondage. Satan must be dealt with. Satan must be conquered and vanquished. And God announced his program for accomplishing that great and mighty end. That, I say again, is the message of the whole Bible from here to the very end.

The Bible is not a book that tells us what we must do to put ourselves right. The Bible is not just a book with an appeal to us to do this, that, or the other, to accept certain ideas and put them into practice. It is not a book that teaches morality or ethics. It is not primarily a book that asks us to do anything. I will tell you what it is—it is a great announcement of what God has done. It is God acting, God coming into the garden to the man and woman in their utter hopelessness. What if he had not done that? Then we would have no gospel. There would be no light. The world would be in darkness at this moment. There would be nothing to say. There would be no hope. But God has come, and God has spoken, and he has revealed a plan and a program.

The Bible is revelation. It is not what man thinks or what man aspires after. It is not what man proposes. It is entirely from God. I know nothing about all this apart from the Bible, and it is sheer impertinence and ignorance and intellectual arrogance to put your mind forward and to say that this part of the Bible is right and that is wrong. It is either all right or it is all wrong. It all hangs together. It is all of a piece. It is divine revelation. I know nothing about God, I know nothing about a way of salvation apart from this, and I am entirely shut up to it. To talk about "modern knowledge" and "recent discoveries" and how things are different now from how they were sixty or seventy years ago—my dear friends, that is so childish that it is not really worth answering. We are concerned with the revelation that the eternal God has been pleased to make. He broke into the tragedy of Eden and spoke, and he is speaking still.

What has God said? Well, here it is: "And I will put enmity between thee and the woman, and between thy seed and her seed; it shall bruise thy head, and thou shalt bruise his heel." That is it. This is true history.

Now the first thing we have to learn from the Bible is that there are two types of history. There is, of course, the history that you can read about in your secular history books. There is the history of philosophy and of thought, the history of art and of culture and of human endeavor. It is all history. But that is only one of two histories. And here the Bible speaks plainly to modern men and women. Their tragedy is that they say that history is the only history. But, thank God, it is not! And I do thank God because all that history, true as it is and wonderful in many ways, gets us nowhere.

I mentioned earlier that I agree entirely with great historians who tell us that history is simply a matter of cycles, that it makes no progress and there is no advance—the cyclical view of history. There is a challenge, and in response I get up and I go on and I become strong and mighty, and at last I conquer. I think that I have arrived and that my descendants will advance upward beyond me. But it does not happen like that. Mighty dynasties, great civilizations, have become lost. This is true of Egypt, Greece, Rome, Spain, and many other nations. They had learning, marvelous knowledge, even scientific knowledge, and great military power. They rose, but they went down again. Why? According to the historians it is simply because having arrived and having conquered, they began to rest on their laurels. They had conquered most of the world perhaps, but other people began to say, "Why should they have it all?" and rose to the challenge in their turn. That is the story of secular history, is it not?

And it is not only true of military conquest, it is equally true of knowledge. Periods of great knowledge have been succeeded by periods of darkness and ignorance. We talk about the Dark Ages in Europe when all the wonderful culture of Greece was entirely lost, and Erasmus and others in the sixteenth century had to rediscover it. I could continue at great length and entertain you with stories on this subject. Have you read how the ancient Chinese knew all about penicillin without giving it that name? They discovered it and were using it. Then that knowledge was lost for many centuries, and now it has come back again.

I can give you an illustration out of my own experience. A research worker, a fellow of the Royal Society, came into my room one day in despair and said, "I'm giving up research work."

"Why?" I asked.

"Well," he replied, "I've worked for six years on a particular problem. I thought I'd made a great discovery. But I went and read a book in the Royal College of Surgeons library, and there, in a footnote, I found that the ancient Egyptians had been doing the very thing that I thought I'd discovered for the first time."

So there it is. Secular history is a matter of cycles. You just go round and round, and you never arrive anywhere. In spite of all the years and all their travail and toil, men and women are still in the same predicament. They are as miserable and as aware of failure as they have ever been.

But, thank God, there is another history, a true history—God initiating a process, raising up a seed who will fight this foul tyrant who has conquered men and women. The promised one is going to vanquish Satan and deliver humanity. This spiritual history runs side by side with the secular history, intermingling with it now and then, intervening in it, and yet always separate. In the history of the Bible these nations are mentioned. Cultures appear here. Greece and Rome and Egypt all come in. Yes, but they are mere incidentals. *The* history here is the carrying out of the purpose of Genesis 3:15: "I will put enmity between thee and the woman, and between thy seed and her seed; it shall bruise thy head, and thou shalt bruise his heel." The Bible is nothing but the outworking of all that. That is its message—how God is vanquishing and destroying the Devil and will ultimately undo all his nefarious work.

God said in effect, "There is the plan." And he said at the very beginning that it would be absolutely certain, that nothing would stop it, nothing would thwart it. I like the word "shall" here: "It [the seed of the woman] *shall* bruise thy head, and thou *shalt* bruise his heel." This is absolute certainty, on the authority of the eternal God.

What, then, has happened? Well, read your Bibles. Go through from beginning to end. Follow it through, keeping your eye on this promise. Do not allow yourself to be lost in the details. Keep your eye on the big story. Follow the red line, if you like. Keep to the theme of salvation. Watch it being worked out. Note the two lines, the two seeds, the conflict. It began at once in two of the sons of Adam and Eve—Abel and Cain. Cain, the representative of Satan, the man full of hate, with murder in his heart, killed his brother. Abel did not hate Cain, but Cain hated Abel. There was conflict from the very beginning.

And on it goes. I am simply giving you a bird's-eye view of the Bible because so many fail to see this, and as a result they do not understand the Christian message. Look at it again in Noah. Noah and his family, just eight people, were saved, and the rest of the world was destroyed. It is the same conflict. The people ridiculed Noah. God had raised him up and made him a preacher of righteousness. He revealed his program to him. Noah believed it and began building his ark. And the people said, "The man's mad. What's he talking about a flood for? He's been saying it for years!"

A hundred years went by, and nothing happened. On the man went with his ark and his preaching, and they resisted him and persecuted him. But you know what happened. It is the same conflict. The seed of the woman; the seed of the serpent.

Hurry on and come to the call of a man whose name was Abram

and see how God called him out of his land. He came from a pagan land and was undoubtedly brought up as a pagan himself. But God called him out and revealed himself to him and said in summary, "You are a part of my program. I am going to do something in you that will eventuate in the coming of the Savior."

Abram, the seed of the woman, turned into Abraham. And out of his loins came the nation of Israel, God's chosen people, the bearers of his oracles, the ones who spoke with his authoritative voice. But they were opposed from within. The Devil even got into the camp of God's people and led them into sin. There was a struggle within the nation as well as with the nations outside. This was nothing but the conflict between the seed of the woman and the seed of the serpent.

Follow this right through. It is such a breathtaking story. There are times when you feel that God will lose. The enemy seems to be triumphant; the children of Israel are almost gone. At times it appears there is nobody left who is a believer. Poor Elijah sitting in a cave said, "And I, even I only, am left" (1 Kings 19:14). But he was wrong. There were another seven thousand!

As you keep reading the story, you ask, what will happen? The seed of the woman is about to be exterminated. The Devil is so mighty. He has such great forces. He is triumphant all along the line. What will happen?

Well, here is the fight and the conflict. It continues on, and people begin to feel hopeless. So God sends them special messengers, called prophets, who say in essence, "It's all right. Hold on. God's purpose is still sure. He is going to send *the* Deliverer. A Messiah will appear."

And the people wait, and the years pass, and the Messiah does not come. But God raises another messenger who says the same thing. And the messengers come one after another. But then there is a terrible four hundred years when there is no word from God. After Malachi there is a dead silence, and people say, "Where's God? What's happening?" The enemy is powerful. There are terrible persecutions, and even Jerusalem and the Holy Land have been conquered by the Roman army. The Devil seems triumphant. It seems that the seed of the serpent has prevailed!

But it has not! "When the fulness of the time was come, God sent forth his Son, made of a woman, made under the law, to redeem them that were under the law" (Galatians 4:4–5). Here is the real seed of the woman. A virgin birth, you see. No man was the father. Jesus was born of a virgin, conceived by the Holy Spirit. The seed of the woman had arrived.

But watch the conflict now! King Herod, as the seed of Satan, tried to kill the seed of the woman when Jesus was an infant. Read again the first chapters of Matthew's Gospel. See the seed of the serpent trying to destroy the promised one, and failing. But the conflict did not end there. Watch Jesus being tempted by the Devil for forty days and forty nights in the wilderness. Keep your eye on the Pharisees and the Sadducees and the scribes. Has there ever been such malevolence, such hatred, such rampant devilry? Read the four Gospels. See how the world treated this Son of God who had come to save, who worked miracles, who was always doing acts of kindness. Look at what they did to him. "He came unto his own, and his own received him not" (John 1:11).

They threw stones at him. They spat in his face. They all joined in a mighty chorus and said, "Away with him! Crucify him! Give us a robber rather than this man." What was this? It was nothing but the enmity between the seed of the serpent and the seed of the woman. The seed of the serpent entered into Judas. He incarnated himself, as it were, in Judas.

And look at the conflict reaching its intensity in that hall of trial when all the powers were set against Jesus and they condemned him. The seed of the serpent was conquering, was he not? They had the Son of God. They were nailing him to the cross. They were killing him. He was expiring. The seed of the serpent had conquered. Are you sure?

What was really happening there? According to the apostle

Paul, it was this: "And having spoiled principalities and powers, he made a show of them openly, triumphing over them in it," on that very cross (Colossians 2:15). He did die, and he was buried. And they thought they had sealed their victory by putting the stone before the mouth of that tomb and sealing it. But he burst asunder the bands of death and arose triumphant over the grave. He went out leaving the death clothes behind as evidence in the tomb. He manifested himself to the people, and he ascended to heaven and sent the Holy Spirit.

What am I talking about? My dear friends, this is the drama of salvation, this is the whole story of the Bible. This is the exposition of what God himself tells us in Genesis 3:15: "It shall bruise thy head, and thou shalt bruise his heel." This is a terrible sight. The Devil is so powerful, so mighty, so strong, so subtle that it takes the power of God to deal with him and to vanquish him. And the victory over the Devil is not possible without this incident, this episode.

"Thou shalt bruise his heel," and the promised one *was* bruised. He died. The Devil thought he had killed him, but he had only bruised his heel. He had forgotten what God had said in Eden. But he did bruise his heel. There is no deliverance from Satan except through the death of Christ. That is how the Savior delivers. His heel was bruised. He suffered. He bore the punishment. He literally tasted death for everyone. But in so doing, he bruised the serpent's head.

Just before his death, our Lord said, "Now is the judgment of this world: now shall the prince of this world be cast out" (John 12:31). On that occasion he gave the Devil a mortal wound from which he will never recover, "that through death," says the author of the Epistle to the Hebrews, "he might destroy him that had the power of death, that is, the devil; and deliver them who through fear of death were all their lifetime subject to bondage" (2:14–15). He robbed the Devil of that power. He has taken the sting out of death.

But the end has not yet come. Since then the victory has been continuing. The sending of the Holy Spirit has had this effect, so that the fight still goes on with a greater intensity, and the gospel, this gospel I am preaching to you, is being preached to tell men and women that the Devil has received that mortal wound and that all who look to Christ and trust in him and believe in him can be taken out of the dominion of Satan and can be rescued and redeemed. "Go and tell them," says the Lord to Paul on the road to Damascus, "that the way is wide-open. They must live in the strength of my victory."

And that message has been preached ever since. When the gospel goes out in the power of the Holy Spirit, it convicts men and women of their bondage to Satan, of their helplessness and hopelessness. It opens their eyes to the salvation that is in Christ, and it brings them out.

And the victory will go on until the day comes when this self-same seed of the woman—the Son of God, the Lord Jesus Christ—comes back, finally, to rout all his enemies. Satan and all who belong to him will be cast into the lake of perdition. Evil and all its vestiges will be burned out of existence. There shall be "new heavens and a new earth, wherein dwelleth righteousness" (2 Peter 3:13), and Satan will finally be destroyed for all eternity.

Jesus shall reign where'er the sun
Does his successive journeys run;
His kingdom stretch from shore to shore,
Till moons shall wax and wane no more.

Isaac Watts, "Jesus Shall Reign"

A day is coming when Satan shall not only be bound but shall be crushed to destruction. Then sin and evil shall be no more. The seed of the woman "shall bruise thy head." God in Christ will finally be completely victorious, and the Devil will be robbed and shorn of all his power and might.

Friends, this is the Christian message. By nature you belong to the Devil. That is why the world is living as it is. That is why it laughs at the gospel and ridicules talk about the blood of Christ. It is blinded by its god, its master, the armed strong man. And this is the terrifying thought: if you die like that, you will go to the same misery, the same destruction, and the same wretchedness as the Devil and all his forces. But if you believe that God sent his own Son into this world to rescue you from that bondage, from those horrid clutches, and to transfer you into his own kingdom and to make you his child and to shower his blessings upon you, you have nothing to fear about the end of the world and the judgment of God. The Devil cannot touch you because in Christ you have already passed from judgment to life.

"He that is begotten of God keepeth himself," writes the apostle John in his first epistle, "and that wicked one toucheth him not. And we know that we are of God, and the whole world lieth in wickedness" (1 John 5:18–19). We belong to God. What is the blood that is in you? What is the seed that is in you? Have you received the divine seed? Have you been born again not of corruptible but of incorruptible seed by the Word of God that lives and abides forever?

My dear friend, this is not something remote. I am talking about you. You are either in the hands of the Devil or you are in the hands of God, and your eternal fate will correspond. But if you are in the hands of the Devil, I plead with you: recognize your position and your condition. Hearken unto this wonderful message about God sending his own Son born of a woman—the seed of the woman—to rescue and redeem you. Cast yourself upon him. Speak to him. Tell him, "Though I cannot see you, I believe you are there. I believe the message. Deliver me!"

He *will* deliver you, and you will be given a new life and a new strength and a new power. You will be enabled to resist the Devil, and you will have the wonderful experience, for the first time in your life, of seeing him fleeing from you because he cannot withstand the name and the blood of the Christ who is now ruling in you.

6

THE CHERUBIM AND
THE FLAMING SWORD

And the LORD God said, Behold, the man is become as one
of us, to know good and evil: and now, lest he put forth his
hand, and take also of the tree of life, and eat, and live for
ever: Therefore the LORD God sent him forth from the garden
of Eden, to till the ground from whence he was taken. So he
drove out the man; and he placed at the east of the garden
of Eden Cherubims, and a flaming sword which turned every
way, to keep the way of the tree of life.

GENESIS 3:22-24

We have seen that the Bible always speaks to us about the
precise condition in which we find ourselves and that it
has a great message that covers the whole of life. And so, without
entering into the details of what is happening in the world today,
the Bible speaks about them in a profound manner that nothing else
can approach.

Nothing, I sometimes think, so proves the truth of the biblical
teaching as the way in which men and women refuse to consider it.
You would think that a time of crisis and turmoil and confusion in
the world would drive them to the Bible, but it does not. They turn
in every other direction; they consider every other possible solution.
And there is only one explanation for that attitude, the one the Bible
itself gives us. Scripture tells us that men and women are spiritually

blind and that to the extent that they do see at all, they see only in a human and materialistic sense. They are blind to the really vital issues, to the unseen powers and forces, and these are, after all, the most important realities. The tragedy of men and women in general is that they only see the visible—they do not see the invisible. Therefore at the present hour they do not see the real cause of their troubles. They think in terms of certain individuals who have done this or that, what they should not have done and what should be done and so on. And they get excited about all that. But these are merely symptoms. It is what cannot be seen by the visible eye, what lies behind all this, that really accounts for all that takes place in the world.

Now the Bible is interested in all that. The Bible is a very old book; it has been in this world for such a long time and has seen many a crisis come and go. The Bible was here during the Second World War. It was here in the First World War. It was here, exactly as it is now, in the time of the Napoleonic Wars when people got so excited and thought that the world had never been in such a situation as it was then. The world is always saying that. Every generation tends to repeat it. But the Bible, as it were, looks through all that and says, you are interested in the manifestations and the symptoms, but the tragedy is that you do not see human nature and life in this world as they are, the problem that keeps on creating these crises. You do not see what turns the world into what you are now seeing, the condition that your grandfathers and great-grandfathers and generations still further back saw in their day. So the Bible says, why will you not come and consider what I have to say, for here is the real and the only answer?

The Bible tells us the answer to the two questions we should all be asking. The first is, why are things as they are? The second is, how can they be put right? That is the whole problem, is it not? It really comes down to that: diagnosis and treatment.

But here lies the rub, the difficulty. The world really does not want to consider that first question. It is only interested in the second. And the world does not like the Bible because it says that you cannot come to the second question unless you have truly understood the first. The Bible stands against us at that very point and says, you cannot have the treatment until you have submitted to the diagnosis.

But the world hates this diagnosis. It says, I'm not interested in that. I don't care what the cause is as long as you can put it right. It is the same with our physical illnesses. When we are suffering an acute pain, the doctor comes and looks at us and asks us a number of questions. Then he begins to examine us, and he puts his hand on us and listens to our heart. Meanwhile, we are saying to ourselves, *Why is this man wasting time? Why doesn't he relieve my pain?* That is a natural human reaction. But the doctor knows very well that until he is fairly clear in his mind as to the cause of your pain, it is very dangerous to attempt to relieve it. But we do not like probing analysis like that found in the Bible. We know what it is going to say about us, and we do not want that. The world today really hates the first part of the gospel; it wants the cure immediately.

In this little paragraph in Genesis that we are now looking at, these two aspects are put before us. What a perfect picture they give us of modern people and the modern world. Look at Adam and Eve. There they are, out in the great wide world in the wilderness of life. They have been driven out of paradise. They have been driven out of the place where they simply had to pick the fruit and eat it. And here they are, alone and isolated, faced with a barren wilderness, at the mercy of all sorts of animals and beasts, not knowing what to do, frustrated and confused, feeling a terrible loneliness, with the problem of life coming down heavily upon them.

Is that not a perfect picture of men and women today? They are confused. They feel they are in a wilderness. They do not understand life. It does not seem to be turning out as they had thought it would. It is not as they would like it to be. But here they are. They cannot help themselves. They find themselves on the outside, always trying to get back somewhere and failing. Let me analyze verses 23–24 in order to bring out the two sides—the diagnosis and the treatment.

There are the man and the woman outside the garden of Eden, driven out by God. But why are they outside? Why should these two, who have known such a perfect life, suddenly find themselves surrounded by problems and difficulties, battling against immensities they do not understand, conscious of having lost something? How have they come into such a position? This is just another way of asking the question, why is the world as it is today?

Here is the first answer. The human race is as it is because man refused to realize at the beginning who and what he is and tried to be something that he was not and was never meant to be. The Scripture puts this in a very brief word: "Therefore the LORD God sent him forth from the garden of Eden, to till the ground from whence he was taken." That is a tremendous statement—"to till the ground from whence he was taken." What a tremendous statement about human beings. What does it tell us? It tells us that man is a created, finite being. That is not the modern view, is it? But that is the truth. Man was taken from the ground. God took some of the dust of the earth, and from that he made man and then breathed his spirit into him. That is man's origin.

But man was not content with that. And the Devil knew it, so he knew exactly what to do. He said to Eve, "Yea, hath God said, Ye shall not eat of every tree of the garden?"

"Well," Eve answered in essence, "we can eat the fruit except from one tree."

"Well," said the serpent, "I'll tell you why he said that. 'For God doth know that in the day ye eat thereof, then your eyes shall be opened, and ye shall be as gods, knowing good and evil.'"

Adam and Eve, of course, jumped to the bait. They accepted the serpent's words at once. They did not like any suggestion that they were finite and were dependent upon God and had to lead a life of obedience. They pulled themselves up to their full height. They were not creatures who had come from the dust. Man is a kind of god! That was their conception. There is no limit to man. Marvelous man! So when the Devil came, they were ready indeed to listen to his suggestion that if only they would disobey God and eat this fruit, they would become—indeed, would then be—*as* God. And they felt they had it in them to stand there and to be equal with God. So they ate the fruit.

That and that alone explains why men and women are as they are today. That is why Adam and Eve were thrust out of the garden. People are as they are because Adam and Eve refused to realize who and what they were and tried to be something they were never meant to be. And the whole story of the human race, the whole history of the world, stems out of that one primary, original, fatal fallacy.

I do not want to dwell too long on this first point, but it is of the very essence of the preaching of the Bible and the gospel to say that the chief trouble of men and women is still their great conceit. The apostle Paul puts that in this way in writing to the Corinthians:

> Ye see your calling, brethren, how that not many wise men after the flesh, not many mighty, not many noble, are called: But God hath chosen the foolish things of the world to confound the wise; and God hath chosen the weak things of the world to confound the things which are mighty; and base things of the world, and things which are despised, hath God chosen, yea, and things which are not, to bring to nought things that are: That no flesh should glory in his presence. (1 Corinthians 1:26-29)

Then the apostle winds it up with a quotation of Old Testament Scripture: "He that glorieth, let him glory in the Lord" (v. 31). In other words, God has made a way of salvation in which human pride, and especially pride of intellect, is humbled and abased.

But, you see, that is the very thing man refused to do at the beginning. That is the thing he still persists in refusing to accept. Fundamentally, man has a false view of himself—of his potentiality, his ability, and his power. He feels that he really is a king or a giant or a genius and that he is capable of anything, and he worships himself. Now I am not exaggerating. I am not overdrawing the picture.

You and I, my dear friends, have the misfortune to be living at a time when we are reaping what has been going on for about a hundred years. There has been a great turning away from God, and it has all been due to the fact that man really began to believe that he was so wonderful that he did not need God. He felt there was nothing he could not do. He could make a paradise, a perfect world. And this ancient fantasy persists. Man forgets that he has come from the ground, from the dust; he hates the idea. But he finds himself constantly groveling in the dust. God keeps on reminding him that he has come from it. So every time man exalts himself, he is stricken down, and there he is licking the dust again. "Therefore the LORD God sent him forth from the garden of Eden, to till the ground from whence he was taken."

I pass from that to my second principle, which is this: all that man obtains in this folly and sin of his apart from God always disappoints him and always leads to further trouble. Here is how the Scripture puts it:

> And the LORD God said, Behold, the man is become as one of us, to know good and evil: and now, lest he put forth his hand, and take also of the tree of life, and eat, and live for ever: Therefore the LORD God sent him forth from the garden of Eden. (Genesis 3:22–23)

Notice that Adam and Eve, as the result of their action in eating of the tree of the knowledge of good and evil, did obtain a knowledge of good and evil. They thought that if they ate of that tree, it would enlighten them, and they would be as gods and would know everything and have knowledge of evil as well as good. That was what they wanted. Before that, they had been ignorant of evil. They had been living in paradise, in perfect communion with God. They had never known anything but blessing. They had not had to work to get food. They had always enjoyed peace and happiness and joy. Until this point their life had been a life of unadulterated joy and bliss. But they thought that this knowledge of evil as well as good would enlarge their scope. So at the suggestion of the Devil, they did what God had told them not to do, and as a result they obtained the knowledge of evil as well as good. But, alas, the moment they put the fruit into their mouths, it became sour. And that is the whole story of the human race—the fruit becoming sour, the coveted knowledge that supposedly was going to make everything perfect turning against those who longed for it.

Now I want to show you how that happened immediately when man sinned and fell. You see, man looked at all these things theoretically, and his position was, *Now I have such a great capacity. There is nothing really that is beyond me. I'm capable of taking it all in and holding on to it all, and I can enjoy it all.*

So man gained the knowledge of evil. Yes, but he discovered that the knowledge of evil that he obtained was not the knowledge of evil that God has. God looks upon both good and evil from the outside, objectively. He looks down upon them. But alas for poor man, his knowledge was not objective. The knowledge he obtained was subjective. And what was that knowledge? It was the knowledge of the fact that the moment he ate that prohibited fruit, he became the slave of evil; he was under the power of evil, under the dominion of Satan and of sin. Yes, he had a knowledge of evil. We all have it. But what is this knowledge? Well, here it is, says the apostle Paul:

> To will is present with me; but how to perform that which is good I find not. For the good that I would I do not: but the evil which I would not, that I do. . . . But I see another law in my members [dragging me down], warring against the law of my mind. (Romans 7:18–19, 23)

I have a knowledge of evil, and you have it, too, do you not? Man wanted the knowledge of evil. Well, this is it. Within us there is a kind of inferno. You are conscious of it, are you not? Every one of us is conscious of some terrible power operating inside us. You wake up in the morning, and before you have had time truly to wake up and to think actively and positively, an evil thought comes to you. You may walk down the street as innocent as a child, as it were, and suddenly you find there is evil within you.

Man did obtain a knowledge of good and evil, but I say again, it is not God's knowledge. God sees evil and hates it and is above it and is going to destroy it. But man has come to know it as an incubus that is upon him, something that grips him not only externally but within. We have an appalling knowledge of evil, every one of us. It is inside us. Man, in seeking it, has found it. But it is not what he had anticipated; it is not what he had expected.

Another part of the knowledge of evil is this—man has not only come to know evil as a great and malevolent influence and power in his life, but he has also obtained a knowledge of it in its evil consequences. And what are these, over and above the ones I have mentioned? Well, here is the first: punishment. Man was thrown out of the garden, shivering in the cold, out in the great wide world without any protection, having to slave and work and labor. That is the consequence. Man had never known that before. You cannot sin without immediately receiving a certain amount of punishment.

A second consequence is remorse. Feeling you have been a fool. Wondering what it was that made you do it again, though you were so miserable the last time you did it. You kick and berate yourself. Remorse. Shame. And accompanying this misery is depression, fear of the future, wondering what is happening, what you can do.

And then, looming at the back of it all and perhaps most terrifying of all, is the certain knowledge that it all leads to death. Man was placed on probation by God; and if he had only obeyed God and continued to obey him, he would never have died. Death would never have come to him. If man had only obeyed God, God would have allowed him to eat of the tree of life, and he would have obtained immortality as a reward. But he took the law into his own hands, and therefore the curse came upon him: "In the day that thou eatest thereof thou shalt surely die" (Genesis 2:17). And the specter of death appeared before him. He was thrown out of the garden, and there he was facing death. It stood far away on the horizon, but it came nearer and nearer. And we are all aware of it.

That, you see, is life as the result of the Fall and the result of sin. That is how it happened at the beginning, and that is how it is still happening. We are all born with this knowledge of sin and of evil. In our way and in our own day and generation we are doing exactly what Adam did. The trouble with man has always been that he has put his faith in knowledge instead of in God; he puts knowledge in the place of God. That is what Adam did, was it not? He said in essence, "If only I can get this knowledge, I won't need God and can afford to disobey God. With this knowledge I will be absolutely complete. I will need nothing further."

I would remind you again that during the last hundred years there has been a great departure from God. You know, by going to a place of worship, we are great exceptions. The vast majority of people do not attend a place of worship. They do not listen to sermons about God. Why not? Well, about a hundred years ago, people decided that knowledge—and especially, of course, scientific knowledge—would render them independent of God. With our latest discoveries and inventions, they argued, we will not need God at all. We'll be able to create heat, and we'll be able to produce artificial rain to fructify our crops. God won't be necessary. People in the past, because of their ignorance, prayed to God for the blessings of the harvest and so on, but we're independent. We've put our faith in science. We've split the atom.

And what is the position at this hour? Is it not just a repetition of what happened at the beginning? The fruit has become very sour again. The knowledge that we thought would solve all our problems is actually our greatest problem of all. The atom we have split, the very knowledge to which we have pinned our faith, constitutes our greatest problem, just as it became the greatest problem for poor Adam and Eve. *Oh,* they must have thought to themselves, *would to God that we had remained in ignorance! Why did we ever ask for this knowledge of evil? Oh, that we had gone on as we were.* But it was too late. They were away from the garden and away from God. Man is so slow to learn that lesson. Do you still feel, my friend, that with all your modern knowledge and learning you have no need of God? Well, that is the sort of thinking that puts man out of paradise and into the howling, barren wilderness.

But that brings me to my next principle, which is this: in spite of all this, man is foolish enough to try to evade the consequences of his own sinful action. He is still trying to clutch at certain blessings that he desires. Here it is put in this form: God said, "Behold, the man is become as one of us." You see there the doctrine of the Trinity, do you not? God is not talking to angels or to men. God the Father and God the Son and God the Holy Spirit are having a conversation among themselves. "Behold, the man is become as one of us, to know good and evil: and now, lest he put forth his hand, and take also of the tree of life, and eat, and live for ever . . ." (Genesis 3:22). Because of that possibility, God decided to drive him out of the garden.

In other words, God knew that man in sin would act in this manner, that though in his folly he had brought calamity upon himself by his disobedience, he would now stretch out his hand and clutch at that tree of life so he could still go on living. Though he was fallen and sinful and had the knowledge of evil, he would continue to defy God. So God sent him away.

It is at that point that I see most clearly of all the parallel between man at the beginning, the moment he fell, and man as he is at this present time. Indeed, I would venture to assert that this one statement is the whole explanation of the history of civilization. Read your history books. Do not just take it from me. Do not only read your Bible—read your secular history books. And do not only read about kings and marriages and births and wars and deaths, read about the history of thought. Go back and read Greek philosophy. Read mythology, and read about people planning their utopias.

What does it all mean? Just this: man thrust out is always trying to get back. He knows that in that garden there is a tree of life, and he wants it. He still will not admit that he is wrong. He will not admit his sin. He will not admit his dependence upon God. He wants to go on in spite of God. He wants to live an independent life that will be an eternal life while leaving God out of consideration. And he has been doing that throughout the centuries.

The whole story of civilization is the history of men and women trying to make a perfect world for themselves without God. And every one of us has done that in our own lives. Everybody in the world today is seeking peace, happiness, joy, life. Yes, but the trouble is that men and women are looking for all that without God. They do not think of God. They do not worship God. They do not pray to God. They have no interest in him at all. They are not interested in the Lord Jesus Christ.

People are trying in every way they can to find life, joy, peace, and happiness on their own, and yet they can never find it. They are always outside. They are trying to banish death. They are trying to conquer the grave itself. They are trying to extend life. The ingenuity, the cleverness, the ability, all this, all along the line, is the attempt to perpetuate humanity without God. But the whole enterprise is tragic folly. And the first great message of the gospel, in a sense, is just to say that this endeavor is utterly impossible.

"Where did you find that?" asks someone.

I find it in the last verse: "So he drove out the man; and he placed at the east of the garden of Eden Cherubims, and a flaming sword which turned every way, to keep [to guard] the way of the tree of life" (v. 24). God knows man, and he knows man in sin. He knew that though he thrust man out, man would say, "If only I could get back there, if only I could get just one piece of fruit from the tree of life, if only I could eat that . . ." He would be constantly trying to get back. So God put the cherubim and the flaming sword to guard the entrance, the way of entry, to the tree of life.

What does this mean? This is the position of humanity today. This is the explanation of the fact that in spite of all the culture and the philosophizing and the thinking and the social action and the politics and the wars of two thousand years and more, men and women are as they are today. They are still outside. They cannot get back. Why not? Cherubim! The flaming sword! Whether you like it or not, my friend, this is a fact. You may be trying to get in, but you will fail, just as all your forebears have failed. No one can get in. The cherubim! The flaming sword!

What does that mean? What are the cherubim? Well, they are there to indicate and to represent the presence and the unapproach-ability of Jehovah God. Go through your Bible and look for every reference to the cherubim, and you will always find that they are used to depict and represent the majesty, the might, the ineffable glory of the presence of God. When God commanded Moses to build the tabernacle in the wilderness, one of the things he told him to make was a box, the Ark of the Covenant. And in that box he was to put the Ten Commandments, the moral law of God. Then on top of the box he was to put a kind of lid, a covering, and on top of that two cherubim made out of gold. This lid was called "the mercy seat," and these two cherubim were looking down upon it. They were, you see, the representation of the holiness of God, that which looks down upon the law of God, the expression of God's holy nature (Exodus 25:1–22).

God put cherubim at the east gate, the entry to the garden of Eden through which he had just expelled Adam and Eve. That means that whenever man tries to come back to obtain this blessing of life and joy and peace, he immediately comes face-to-face with God, the everlasting and eternal God, the God who is light and in whom is no darkness at all. Read of the men who have come any-where near him or have seen just a glimpse of his glory. They fall down. They are helpless. They do not know what to do with them-selves. The cherubim represent the ineffable glory of God.

And what else? Consider the flaming sword that turned every which way. If you suddenly see it on the left and think you can slip by on the right, it is there before you can move. It is turning every-where, and you will never escape it or avoid it. This, my dear friend, is nothing but the wrath of God against sin. And there is nothing more vital for us all to realize than that. Do you want life? Do you want happiness and peace and joy? Do you want to know that you can have an endless life that nothing can touch or destroy? Are these the blessings you are seeking? Very well, I say to you that you will never have them until you have passed God and his wrath against sin. He is there facing you, at the only way of entrance, and the blessings you seek are behind him. You have to get past the sword of God's wrath.

The final tragedy, the final folly of man in sin, is that throughout the centuries he has been trying to find life in his own strength. He has looked to learning. He has looked to ability. He has looked to morality. He has looked to a thousand and one things. And he has always failed. Why? Because these cannot deal with the sword. They cannot get past God.

"Well," says someone, "do you just want to condemn us and tell us all that we're hopeless and lost? Is the message of Christianity that individually and as a world we are doomed? Are you saying there is no way to life and peace and joy and all of which I stand in need?"

Thank God, that is not my message. I want to tell you that there is a way into that garden. There is only one way, but there is that one. The author of the Epistle to the Hebrews tells us about it:

> Having therefore, brethren, boldness to enter into the holiest by the blood of Jesus, *by a new and living way*, which he hath consecrated for us, through the veil, that is to say, his flesh ... Let us draw near with a true heart in full assurance of faith, having our hearts sprinkled from an evil conscience. (10:19–20, 22)

What does this mean? There is only one way to obtain these blessings, and it is a way that has discovered the method of somehow or other standing in the presence of the glory of God without being consumed. That is absolutely essential. There is no entry into that garden, into that paradise where the blessings of God are still to be found, unless somehow we can stand before the glory of God and not shrivel into nothing. And it is possible.

There is one, and only one, who can stand in the presence of God and look into his face of glory. He is the Son of God, who is God himself, who shares the same glory but who, blessed be his name, came down into this world and took human nature upon himself, who was made flesh and dwelt among us. He came outside into the wilderness; he came out himself. He need not have come. He was not driven out as man was. He came out voluntarily. He asked if he might come out, and the Father sent him. And he came to us in the wilderness and took our nature upon himself. He identified himself with us. He came as man, and now he stands as man, the God-man, and looks into the face of God. No one else could. Every saint in the Old Testament failed. No one can ever look into the face of God and live. No human being can see God and live. But here is one who can because he is God as well as man.

"Ah, yes," you say, "that's all right. But what about the sword?"

Well, my dear friend, this is the most marvelous thing of all. The Son of God advanced against the flaming sword, and it smote him, and it killed him. It broke his body, and in breaking his body it broke itself. Now the way is opened into the paradise of God, to the tree of life, to salvation and all its indescribable blessings. Did you notice how this is expressed in Hebrews: "By a new and living way, which he hath consecrated for us, through the veil, that is to say, his flesh [his body]" (10:20)? He advanced, I say, on the sword, and he said, "Smite me." And in smiting him, it smashed itself.

Through the broken body and the shed blood of the Son of God, you and I can enter into that paradise from which man was expelled. And we can take of the tree of life and eat abundantly of it. In the Communion service, the bread represents his body, and the wine represents his blood. That is why we have the Communion service. It is not mere custom or sham or just a happy picture. There is no way into the paradise of God except through Jesus Christ and him crucified. If he had not taken that smiting with the sword, there would never have been an opening, though he is the Son of God. It was not enough for the Son of God to come into the world. It was not enough for him to teach us. It was not enough for him to live perfectly and to give us an example. Before we can enter, the sword must do its work. And it has done it. Isaiah, eight hundred years before it actually happened, was shown this by the Holy Spirit: "Yet we did esteem him . . . smitten of God" (Isaiah 53:4). Peter says, "by [his] stripes ye were healed" (1 Peter 2:24). He took it all upon himself.

So for all who believe in the Lord Jesus Christ, the entrance is no longer blocked. In Christ we can face God; we can have boldness to enter into the holiest of all by the blood of Jesus. Not by myself. No, for I am a vile sinner. But I am in him. I enter by his obedience. He kept the law perfectly, not only for himself, but for all who believe in him.

> *The terrors of law and of God*
> *With me can have nothing to do;*
> *My Savior's obedience and blood*
> *Hide all my transgressions from view.*

Augustus Toplady[6]

Do you want life, life that is life indeed, life abundant, life that will take you through death to eternity and glory? Do you want peace, joy, and happiness? My dear friend, give up trying to obtain them in your own strength or in the strength of any human knowledge. They have all failed. There is only one way. It is Jesus Christ and him crucified. You must pass through him and in him into the presence of God who is ever ready to receive all who come to him by Jesus Christ.

7

GOD MUST PUNISH SIN

And the LORD said, I will destroy man whom I have creat-
ed from the face of the earth; both man, and beast, and the
creeping thing, and the fowls of the air; for it repenteth me
that I have made them. But Noah found grace in the eyes of
the LORD.

GENESIS 6:7-8

It is my intention to deal with this great and important incident, the account of which, in part, is found in the sixth chapter of the book of Genesis. I want to look at the incident as a whole in order that we may learn the vitally important message that it has to teach us. It deals with two fundamental questions. The first is, what is the cause of the trouble in the world? The second question is, what can be done about it?

Now men and women are very concerned about the problems in the world—at least, those who think at all are. And it seems to me that the majority do think, but unfortunately they keep their eyes at a certain level only and refuse to consider the message of the Bible. As we have been seeing, the Bible speaks to us about life itself, and it is because people fail to realize this that they are not interested in this book. They regard religion merely as a subject for academic study, a matter of interest only to those who are drawn in that direction. I remember once attending a conference at which I had been asked to be the chaplain for the week. I found that in the almost endless list of subjects that would be dealt with at that conference, religion was number 16. People had come there to study literature and music and art, but only a few wanted to study religion.

Many hold the view that religion is a theoretical matter to be taken up as a hobby. People have all sorts of hobbies, and this is one of them. And, further, it is thought that the number who are interested in the study of religion is becoming smaller year by year. There are still a few, but for the vast majority religion is outdated, outmoded; it has nothing to say and is completely irrelevant.

But we are starting from the basis that not only is this book relevant but that it alone is relevant. We have spent several chapters on the third chapter of the book of Genesis, and our whole object has been to show that we really do not even begin to understand the nature of the problem of the modern world until we accept the message of that chapter, for there and there alone is the real explanation. Try all the other explanations if you like, but you will find every one of them to be inadequate. Here alone is an explanation that fits the facts. Here we see that people are as they are and the world is as it is because of man's rebellion against God, because man has set himself up as the authority and has spurned the divine voice.

Now we have been seeing that Adam and Eve's rebellion immediately led to some terrible consequences, which are still with us. In Genesis 3 we are given an accurate description of life today. Man brought his misery upon himself. He deliberately, voluntarily, put himself under the dominion of his archenemy, the archenemy of God; he put himself into the power of the Devil, Satan, the god of this world, the prince of the power of the air. And he has remained in that bondage ever since, unable to do anything about it. He has tried throughout the centuries to break free, but he has never succeeded. He never will.

But thank God, as we have seen, it is just there that the message of the gospel comes in. The Bible tells us that in spite of all this, God is still concerned and still cares. The God who looked at Adam and Eve after they had sinned and fallen and who came down into the garden to speak to them is still the same God. That is the message of this book. He came down, you remember. He pronounced judgment upon Adam and Eve and their sin, he showed them the consequences that had to follow, but he did not stop at that. He showed them a way out. He was going to introduce a way of salvation. He was going to set enmity, he said, between the seed of the woman and the seed of the serpent (Genesis 3:15). It would be a mighty warfare in which the serpent's head would be bruised and the seed of the woman would receive a wound in his heel.

That is the message of the Christian gospel, and we find it way back in the third chapter of the book of Genesis. But that is only the beginning. The Bible does not end at the third chapter of Genesis. It goes on, and we have this mighty volume. What is it all about? It is further history. It is the account of the outworking of this plan of God. It is the subsequent record of what God has continued to do with men and women.

And we come, in this sixth chapter of Genesis, to another remarkable incident. After the events that we have been considering, there seems to have been an interval in which God appeared to be doing very little. God seemed to have left humanity to itself. He allowed men and women to go on living in their own way. For many years there was not very much direct intervention. But then suddenly this incident came. God was intervening again; he was doing something again. The God who came down into the garden was again addressing men and women.

That has been the pattern of God's dealing with humanity ever since the Fall. It is vital, it seems to me, that we should be clear about this because, as I am suggesting, it is the only way to understand history. The Bible, I repeat, is a book of history. That is what makes it so practical. It records the actual history of individual men and women and nations. It shows everything in detail in the light of God's overruling in it all and bringing things to pass. In other words, we cannot really understand the history of the world unless we accept the teaching of this book, and not only the world in Bible times. We cannot understand history since the end of the New

Testament canon until now unless we accept the great principles that are laid down here. God has a method of dealing with humanity, and it is always the same method.

On Armistice Sunday[7] we think about wars. We have had two in this [twentieth] century. We have gone through a terrible and a trying period. The whole situation is still problematical and uncertain, and the questions we are all asking are: Why are things like this? Why must they be like this? What is the matter? What can be done about it?

You are familiar with the world's answers. They are put before us in the newspapers and in the journals day by day, week by week, and month by month. But I ask you, are you satisfied with what they are saying? Do these seem to be sufficient answers? Do they hold out any hope for you?

So I am asking you now to consider this message from God. It is not my message or my theory. I am not giving you the result of my deliberations and cogitations. No, no. I am trying simply to expound this book, this message. It is my only authority. Ultimately I know nothing about God apart from what the Bible tells me. I believe that I can deduce God from nature and creation—I happen to believe these proofs of the being and the existence of God—but they are not enough for me. I cannot arrive at any knowledge of the character of God from creation. I can, as Paul reminds the Romans, discover something about his eternal power and creatorship (1:20), but I will never get to know him that way. That brings me to an unknown God. If I am to understand history and myself and to have any hope, I must come to know God. And I have no knowledge of God apart from that which I find in this book where God has been pleased to reveal himself—his character, his person, his purposes, his ideas, his activities.

Here, then, we come across a pattern. God seems to leave the world to itself for long periods, and then he makes himself manifest. He does something. He intervenes. He speaks. We have one example of that in this sixth chapter of the book of Genesis. And the message, I say again, is that God is still the same, that though he may appear to be silent, he is still there, and his purpose is still absolutely certain. The critical periods are there to call attention to that fact. They are the signposts that God himself sets up. And he does it in his love and in his compassion. We are all so dull, and so ready to forget, that God has to remind us in a forcible manner. He has to indicate and point the way. So we have tremendous incidents such as the Flood, the destruction of Sodom and Gomorrah, the destruction of the city of Jerusalem, the captivity of Babylon—certain climactic events. They stand out in this record, in this history. They are all, in a sense, exactly the same. They all have the same message. And nothing is more important for us than that we should learn the lesson that they bring to us.

So, then, what is the lesson of the Flood? I am not going to detain you with a discussion about whether or not the Flood actually happened. I believe it did, and I can give you my reasons. I am familiar with everything that has been said against it and have considered the arguments. Nevertheless, I assert that this is history. Let me give you just one reason—and I would accept it for this one fact alone—the Lord Jesus Christ himself said that the Flood took place, and I shall remind you of his teaching. So if you reject this as history, then you are left with the problem of the veracity of the person of the Lord Jesus Christ.

You cannot play fast and loose with these early chapters of Genesis. It is not quite as simple as some people seem to think. They say, "Of course, we no longer believe that. Science has proved this and that." But science, of course, has proved nothing of the kind. What people really mean is that certain scientists have stated their opinions, which is very different. Their opinions are pure theory and supposition. They cannot prove anything at all with regard to whether or not this is history. What they do not realize is that if you reject the historicity of the Flood, you cannot hold on to Jesus Christ and the gospel because he believed that this was literal history.

It is not immaterial, therefore, to ask whether this or any of the other illustrations are historical. It is as material as it is to know that Jesus of Nazareth was born of a virgin, that he worked miracles, that he died and was buried but literally rose again in the body. The facts are absolutely essential. I have no gospel apart from these facts, and the Bible makes a great deal of them. It warns us against the scoffers who laugh at them and say such things as, "Where is the promise of his coming?" (2 Peter 3:4).

Let us go on, then, and see what this account of the Flood has to teach us. Fortunately, there are several references to the Flood in the New Testament, so we are not left to ourselves in this matter. Take, for instance, the account in Luke 17, where our Lord says:

> And as it was in the days of Noah, so shall it be also in the days of the Son of man. They did eat, they drank, they married wives, they were given in marriage, until the day that Noah entered into the ark, and the flood came, and destroyed them all. (vv. 26–27)

There is also a reference to this in the eleventh chapter of the Epistle to the Hebrews. In that great gallery of the saints of the Old Testament we read:

> By faith Noah, being warned of God of things not seen as yet, moved with fear, prepared an ark to the saving of his house; by the which he condemned the world, and became heir of the righteousness which is by faith. (v. 7)

Another reference to the Flood is found in the first epistle of Peter, where we are told that the Lord Jesus Christ was "put to death in the flesh, but quickened by the Spirit: By which also he went and preached unto the spirits in prison; which sometime were disobedient . . . in the days of Noah" (3:18–20). And the apostle goes on to compare Christian salvation to the ark that saved Noah and his family.

There is a final reference in the second epistle of Peter, where the apostle takes up the whole question of the scoffers who were saying, "Where is the promise of his coming?" (3:4). "You've preached to us," they said in effect, "and you've told us that the Lord Jesus

Christ is coming back to judge the world. Well, where is he? Years are passing, and he doesn't come. You can't frighten us. We don't believe that kind of teaching. Where is the promise?"

"Ah," says Peter, "wait a minute. People were like that in the days of the Flood. When Noah preached to them, they ridiculed him. They scorned him. But the Flood came." And then he goes on to say that judgment is coming. It will not be a flood the next time. God promised that he would never drown the world again. He gave a sign of that promise in the rainbow in the heavens. But though he will never drown the earth, he will deal with sin. There will be a judgment. The elements will burn and melt with fervent heat in that final cataclysm that is still to come.

So in the light of all these comments in the New Testament, we can go back to this ancient history and consider its message. What is it? I would divide it like this: there is a general message and a particular message. I shall not dwell on the first point, but I must note it in passing.

The general message is that all calamities are due to sin. God made the world perfect. He placed the man and woman in paradise. And if they had obeyed, it would have continued like that. There would never have been any wars. There would never have been anything to disturb the even tenor of their days and their enjoyment of life and of God. Are we all clear about that, I wonder? Why are there wars? Is there anything more idiotic, more insane, more futile, more harmful to the lot of man? A war is a calamity and always leads to endless trouble in every respect. Where does it come from? The Bible tells us that it has come from sin. It was as a result of the entry of sin that Cain became jealous of his brother Abel and decided to murder him. There it is, and it is still with us, in all the relationships of life. All calamity is the result of sin and would never have come but for sin.

A second principle that seems to me to be equally clear is that God sometimes brings calamity as a punishment for sin. That is the whole message of this incident of the Flood. It was God himself who decided to do this. He said, "And behold, I, even I, do bring a flood of waters upon the earth" (Genesis 6:17). God deliberately decided to do that because of the conditions that prevailed. Now God does not always do that. As I have said, there are long epochs and periods, sometimes apparently lasting for a millennium and more, when God seems to tolerate things. He allows them to take their course and does not seem to do anything about them, so that scoffers say, "Where is your God? Can your God do anything? If he can, why doesn't he? You say he's almighty. But we've forgotten him. We've ignored him. We live our own lives, and nothing happens to us. Everything's going well."

As the psalmist put it, "Thou thoughtest that I [God] was altogether such an one as thyself" (Psalm 50:21). We do not understand his ways. Isaiah says, "For my thoughts are not your thoughts, neither are your ways my ways, saith the LORD" (Isaiah 55:8). His thoughts and ways are as far above us as the heavens are above the earth, higher than our understanding. But God gives us teaching, and it seems to be this: God allows things to go on until they reach a certain climax, and when they do, he acts. And that is what he did in the Flood.

Later on in this same book of Genesis, we read that God said he would not do anything yet, "for the iniquity of the Amorites is not yet full" (Genesis 15:16). Then he would act. You remember God's patience with the city of Nineveh, to which he sent the prophet Jonah. He had waited. He had postponed and appealed. But they did nothing. He allowed the time to pass. But then in his own time he acted. And, of course, that is the great lesson of the Old Testament about the children of Israel. God gave them his laws, and he told them that if they obeyed him, he would bless them, but that if they disobeyed him, he would punish them. Then they began to sin and to disobey God. And they thought something was going to happen at once, but it did not.

"Ah," they said, "everything is all right." And on they went in sin. God sent a messenger to warn them. They paid no attention but continued in sin. Another messenger came; still they paid no attention. And at last they said, "Let's be at ease in Zion. Nothing will ever go wrong for us." Then suddenly God acted.

That is the message. It is the whole history of the Old Testament. And it came to a terrifying climax in A.D. 70 in the destruction of Jerusalem and the casting out of the nation of Israel and its people among the nations of the world. There is the principle. God does not always act at once: he will act, but in *his* own time.

The third general principle is this: every one of these individual calamities in history is nothing but a picture of the final calamity. Every one of them points forward. This is not my theory. It is the teaching of the Bible itself. What is proclaimed is that God will punish sin. I am sorry, my friends, but I say again that I am not trying to tell you what I like or what I think. The whole message of the Bible is that God is just and holy and righteous and pure. I do not hesitate, with reverence, to put it like this: God must punish sin. He cannot deny himself. He cannot go back on his own nature and on his own character. God and sin are eternal incompatibilities. So God pronounces that he must punish sin, and punish it he will. He will punish it in the individual. He will punish it in groups. He will punish the whole world in sin. That is the general message.

Now let me say something about this in particular. Why does God punish sin? The answer is that it is because of what sin leads to, what it produces. God pronounced here that he would destroy that ancient world. Why? Here is the answer in the fifth verse: "And God saw that the wickedness of man was great in the earth, and that every imagination of the thoughts of his heart was only evil continually" (Genesis 6:5). That is why God acted as he did. He saw that the wickedness of the earth was great. That is what always produces God's punishment.

Do not misunderstand me. I am not suggesting to you that the sixth chapter of Genesis is an exact description of the world today, though it may be. God knows, the world is much too much like that at this present moment. But I am not saying that the end of the world is at hand. Again, it may be. I cannot say it is not; I cannot say it is. I am not claiming to understand the times and the seasons. All I know is that there will be an end, and I find this principle in the Scripture: God tolerates iniquity until it reaches a certain climax.

And then he acts. I simply ask you to face the evidence seriously and soberly. It was when God saw that wickedness was great on the earth that he sent the Flood.

God saw also that "every imagination of the thoughts of his [man's] heart was only evil continually" (v. 5). This means that men and women not only did things that were wrong, they delighted in them. They boasted of them. Evil was not merely present in practice but was in the heart, in the imagination, in the mind. There are times in the history of the world when men and women have been evil in practice, but they do not seem to have been devilish in their minds to the extent that they have been at other times. But at this time of the Flood, as someone once put it, the world had reached a new low in iniquity. People's very minds were fiendish. They perverted all their powers and faculties simply to revel in sin.

There is always sin in the world. There was a great deal of sin in the world a hundred years ago. In the Victorian period people committed sinful acts. There was drunkenness. There was immorality. Yes, but I think you will all agree that there is a striking difference between the world then and the world now. When you look into the realm of the mind and the imagination, do you not see the difference? Have you noticed, for instance, the striking difference between Victorian novels and the novels of today? In those days, there was not all this filth. Something new has come in. The imagination, the mind, the thinking, the heart are going down. Music is debased. It is becoming primitive and suggestive. It is no longer as clean as it was. Everything is perverted and twisted. It is happening in literature. It is happening in art. Compare the art of a hundred years ago with that of today. What is this new thing that has come in? Is it not because the imagination and the mind and the heart are becoming evil continually? That is the sort of thing that happened at the time of the Flood. Iniquity and evil and wickedness and vice were rampant.

Then we are told in the eleventh verse, "The earth also was corrupt before God, and the earth was filled with violence." "Corrupt." Polluted. Foul and tarnished. It does not take much imagination to see what that means, does it? You find a description of the same thing in the second half of Paul's first chapter of his Epistle to the Romans. There have been other times when the world was like that. Sodom and Gomorrah were corrupt, low, and full of violence. This verse refers not only to murder and theft and robbery with violence, but to innocent people being attacked, to violence in the manifestation of thoughts such as lust and passion. And again, is this not far too much in evidence in this modern world? The world is much more violent than it was fifty years ago. There has always been violence, but not in this widespread sense. The whole way of life is becoming loud and harsh and cruel and angry. There is a violence about man. He does not fight the way he used to. He has mighty bombs now that will kill thousands, perhaps millions, at a time. Violence! It is here now, and it was there then.

But the trouble with all this is that it is seen by God: "The earth also was corrupt *before God*, and the earth was filled with violence." This is the essence of sin. It was all happening before God, but the world ignored him. It said, "There is no God. And if there is a God, well, it doesn't matter. He can't do anything. He's quite helpless. He doesn't have any power at all." And the people went on living like that under the very eye of God, with God looking down upon them, though they did not believe that. Those are the conditions in which God acts. Those are the kind of conditions that lead to calamities. It is when the world is in such a state that everything goes wrong and men and women are alarmed and terrified and begin to ask, "What's going to happen next?"

But let us not forget that when our Lord spoke about the time before the Flood, he said, "They were eating and drinking, marrying and giving in marriage . . . and knew not until the flood came" (Matthew 24:38–39). Do you see what he is describing? It is a purely materialistic outlook. Eating and drinking, marrying and giving in marriage—this is the only life, this is the only world. So let's get the most out of it. Let's live for it entirely. Don't talk about God. Don't talk about eternity. Don't talk about death. Don't talk about judgment. Just live for the present, for enjoyment, for happiness. That was the picture, and it is the order of the day now. They were like that before the Flood, says our Lord, and that was why God visited them in judgment. They were living purely on the earthly level. They only thought of themselves, and they lived for themselves. That was what they wanted—plenty to eat, plenty to drink. "Let's get more money so we can enjoy ourselves. It doesn't matter what happens. Sufficient unto the day is the evil thereof. Let's eat, drink, and be merry."

I am not applying this to the age in which we live. I am leaving that to you. But I cannot help noting the terrible and terrifying parallel, the apparent utter unconcern of men and women in spite of what they have already experienced. Would you not have thought that two world wars would have sobered everyone? That they would have been forced to stop and to say, "We can't go on like this. There must be something wrong somewhere. What is it?" But are they doing that? Do the radio and television programs suggest that they are? It is just over ten years since the last world war ended with a horrifying atomic bomb. And yet men and women today are thinking about everything else, about eating and drinking and having their supposedly good time and laughing at the jokes of the comedians. "How funny it all is! Things are going well. Let's enjoy ourselves. The money's coming in. People are warning us, but why listen to that? Why be a spoilsport? Let's carry on as we are." It is precisely the same mentality as in Genesis 6.

Now those were the conditions that led God to act. Having seen all this, he gave his warning. Listen to what he said: "My spirit shall not always strive with man, for that he also is flesh: yet his days shall be an hundred and twenty years" (Genesis 6:3). What does that mean? Well, that is God's warning to men and women in this condition. God is saying, "Look here, I am not going to restrain you much longer. I am not going to tolerate this much longer. I will give you another 120 years, and then, unless you have repented, I will act."

The narrative puts it as an anthropomorphism, which means that God speaks to us in a way that we can understand. He says, "For it repenteth me" (v. 7). God does not repent. God does not change his mind. Why, then, does he use this term? He wants us to understand. This is his way of pronouncing judgment. He expresses his opinion on men and women. He expresses abhorrence and detestation at their way of living.

So God warns sinners. God always warns. He warns us individually, and he warns the whole world. You have within you what is called the conscience, and every time you are confronted by temptation, it speaks, it warns. You have never sinned without being warned; never. You were told of the consequences, and yet you did it. God always warns before he strikes. The Bible is nothing but a great book of warning. It warns that this righteous God will judge us one by one and that he will "judge the world in righteousness by that man whom he hath ordained" (Acts 17:31)—his own Son, our Lord and Savior, Jesus Christ.

Beloved friend, have you heard the word of warning? Are you happy to go on living as you are and to ignore this message? Armistice Day reminds us of our mortality; it reminds us of death and of the brief span of our existence in this world. You are going out of this world someday. Where are you going? To what are you going? God, I say, warns you. He warns you in the record of the Flood. He warns you in the whole teaching of the Bible. You must stand before him, and he will judge you in righteousness.

God warned the people of that day. And in warning them, he called them to repentance. He told Noah to build the ark. It was a tremendous enterprise, and it took Noah about 120 years to build it. When he began, people said, "What are you doing, man?" And Noah replied in effect, "God is going to judge the world unless we all repent. He's going to drown the world, and he told me to build an ark to save myself and my family."

The people thought it was the funniest joke they had ever heard. How awful! And they came back to him in ten years' time and said, "Do you still believe that, Noah? Ten years have gone by, and nothing's happened." On they went—twenty, thirty, forty, one hundred, one hundred and ten, one hundred and nineteen years. "It's really very amusing, isn't it?" they mocked.

Noah preached to them by building the ark, and he preached to them in words. He is described in 2 Peter 2:5 as "a preacher of righteousness." I have already quoted Peter's words in 1 Peter 3:18–20, where Peter says that Christ himself in the spirit was preaching through Noah to those people before the Flood. Noah warned them. He said that God had spoken to him, that God would destroy the world unless they repented. He told them to repent, to believe. He repented himself. He believed. He built the ark. He carried out God's instructions in detail: "Thus did Noah; according to all that God commanded him, so did he" (Genesis 6:22).

Nevertheless, these people paid no attention. They went on eating and drinking, marrying and giving in marriage, "and knew not" what they were doing, said Jesus (Matthew 24:39). They just went on as if nothing was happening. They could not see the signs. They did not believe Noah. They took no notice of the ark. As I have already reminded you, it alarms and terrifies my soul to observe that even the two horrible wars that we have endured [World War I and World War II] have not sobered people. They seem to have made no difference at all. The world is giving itself to pleasure more than ever. Never has this country been so self-satisfied. It is folding its arms. It is having a marvelous boom. We are in a time of great prosperity. We must have our pleasures, whether we can afford them or not. We will buy them on a credit system, though we cannot afford to do so. Eating, drinking, marrying and giving in marriage—all the warnings are ignored, the voice of God is spurned. But God is carrying out his judgment. They "knew not," says the Son of God himself, "until the flood came, and took them all away."

The fact that you and I may ignore the warnings of God will make no difference to God's plan.

Though the mills of God grind slowly,
Yet they grind exceeding small.

Friedrich von Logau;
translated by Henry Wadsworth Longfellow

"One day is with the Lord as a thousand years, and a thousand years as one day" (2 Peter 3:8). God seems to be asleep. Vast epochs pass, and he does nothing, and the world says that he cannot do anything. But the Flood came. Sodom and Gomorrah were destroyed. The children of Israel were conquered by their enemies and were carried away captive; eventually their city was destroyed, and they were thrown out among the nations. God, I say, is warning us in all these events.

And I believe that God is warning us in this century by the state of the world, by the calamity of wars. He has allowed all this for us to see. He is reminding us of the final judgment that cannot be evaded, which no one will be able to avoid. The coming of Christ to judge the world in righteousness is as certain as the Flood, as certain as the birth of Christ as a babe in Bethlehem, as certain as the resurrection of Jesus. It is coming; it must come. God has pledged his word.

And there is only one way of escape. We see it is in Genesis 6:7–8.

> And the LORD said, I will destroy man whom I have created from the face of the earth; both man, and beast, and the creeping thing, and the fowls of the air; for it repenteth me that I have made them. But Noah found grace in the eyes of the LORD.

Noah was not overwhelmed in the calamity but was delivered and was made safe. He "found grace." Why?

The answer is given in the ninth verse where we read, "Noah was a just man and perfect in his generations, and Noah walked with God." That is the secret. The one thing that marked this man out from all the rest was simply that he believed the word of God— nothing else. God came to him and spoke to him, and Noah believed him. That is why he is described as a preacher of righteousness. That is why the eleventh chapter of Hebrews says that he "became heir of the righteousness which is by faith" (v. 7). It was not even his character that saved him. It was that he walked with God. This means that he allowed God to lead him, that he went where God went, that he listened to God and said yes to God. God spoke, and Noah said, "I believe." That is what saved him.

The apostle Peter tells us that as that ark saved Noah from the waters of the Flood, even so belief in the Lord Jesus Christ and being in him will save us from the wrath to come at the final day of judgment of the whole world (1 Peter 3:21). Christ is the ark. Christ is the Savior. Christ is the refuge. God has built his own ark for us, and we only have to enter in by faith. We shall be safe when the world is burning and melting and all that is opposed to God is destroyed everlastingly out of his sight.

It all comes to this: we must believe God. If you believe God now, the grace of God will deliver and save you. And what God says is just this—our sinfulness deserves the very selfsame punishment that he meted out to those people in the Flood and will mete out at the end of the world. He pronounces judgment upon sin in every shape and form, and we are all sinners before him. There is just one way of escape—to believe that, to acknowledge it, to stop defending yourself, to stop trying to argue against it with your science or your knowledge or anything else. It is to believe the simple word of God, as Noah did, the word about yourself, that you are a sinner, to confess it and acknowledge it, to repent before God. Then believe him further when he tells you that he has prepared the ark, that he sent his only begotten Son to bear your sins and their punishment. If you believe that and enter into him, your sins will be all blotted out, and you will be safe in life and safe in death and safe through all eternity.

"But Noah" (Genesis 6:8)—is that you? Do you belong to Noah and his family? Are you a child of faith? Do you believe God? If you do, the "but" applies to you, and the grace of God will redeem you and rescue you. Then when the world is dissolving in the last calamity, you will be safe in the arms of Jesus, and you will enter a glory that shall never end. May God open our eyes to the message of the Flood.

8

BABEL:
THE TRAGEDY OF MAN

*And the whole earth was of one language, and of one speech.
And it came to pass, as they journeyed from the east, that
they found a plain in the land of Shinar; and they dwelt there.*

GENESIS 11:1-2

In our study of the opening chapters of Genesis, our whole contention has been that the Bible, far from being remote from life, is the only book that really does deal with life as it is, the only book that gives us anything approximating to an adequate answer to the various questions that we all feel must of necessity be faced at a time like this. Why is the world as it is? That is the basic question. Why the confusion, the trouble, the discord, the misunderstanding with all the consequent unhappiness and misery and wretchedness?

Now it is no use proceeding to consider what can be done about all this until we are perfectly clear as to the cause. I take it that needs no demonstration. I am assuming that no one is foolish enough to say that diagnosis does not matter, that all we need is a little relief. It is nothing but sheer lunacy to medicate symptoms only, to give temporary, passing relief and yet ignore the disease that is causing the symptoms. That is, incidentally, also a thoroughly dishonest thing to do. There are people who say, "Oh, I can't be bothered about causes and explanations. All I know is that I'm in trouble and want relief." Those who say that are the kind of people who make the complete round of all the cults and all the rival philosophies and teachings, only to be disappointed by one after the other. The butterfly attitude toward life is always fatal. No, no, the essence of wisdom is to discover the cause of the problems. And whether we like it or not, the Bible always emphasizes that.

We have seen that God made man perfect and that things went wrong because man rebelled against him. We see this in the third chapter of Genesis. But thank God, before we left that chapter we were able to see that into the midst of the mess and the ruin that man had brought upon himself came God with a promise and a message of salvation. But the tragedy of history—and it is still the tragedy of the world today—is that man will not look at the salvation God offers. Man is prepared to clutch at every will-o'-the-wisp, to put his faith in anything that is offered him, however insubstantial and however lacking in authority, rather than believe the teaching that we have in this book. With a prejudice, a fatal prejudice, he dismisses the Bible. It must be wrong, he says, because it is so old and because we know so much now that was not known when the Bible was written.

Man brought ruin upon himself and was thrown out of the garden. Then you remember the subsequent history. God had given the message, but man again turned away and followed his own devices. In our last study we saw how life became so appalling, so vile, so foul that God visited terrible judgment upon the world in the Flood. He destroyed the ancient world, rescuing and redeeming just one family of eight people.

So after the Flood there was a new start, a new opportunity. But, alas, the chapters following that sixth chapter of Genesis and coming right up to the eleventh chapter show us very clearly that men and women had still not learned the lesson. The seed of that old enmity to God was still there, leading to the same follies. The world goes on repeating itself. It never does anything new. This is amazing. It is astounding. In each of our studies, we have seen without exception that we have been looking at the modern world.

In other words, men and women refuse to learn the lesson; they go on repeating the same old error.

Now we have arrived at another vitally important stage. The theme of the Bible, I would remind you again, is God working out his plan of salvation, God doing what he had promised in the garden of Eden. He said that he would set enmity between the seed of the woman and the seed of the serpent and that there would be warfare without intermission, a terrible war that would culminate in the seed of the woman bruising the serpent's head and his own heel being bruised. And the Bible shows us the various steps and stages along this path.

Here in this eleventh chapter of Genesis, in the tremendous story of what happened at the Tower of Babel, we again come to one of the climactic points, one of the great turning points, in the story. All the intervening history, of course, is of great importance, but I am simply picking out the outstanding events and incidents that have a unique and exceptional significance for us. Here in Genesis 11 we are face-to-face with the explanation of the confusion and conflict between the nations. And, of course, what is true between nations is true within each nation. We as a nation join together against another nation, and they do the same with respect to us. But among ourselves there are conflicts and divisions and confusions. It is the same in principle, but in Genesis 11 the light is thrown onto the nations.

There is no need to point out how contemporary this message is. A conference is now going on in Geneva at which the nations are trying to settle their disagreements. It is one of a series of conferences. They have been going on for years. Indeed, this is, in a sense, the whole story of humanity and of civilization. They are trying to resolve their conflicts, trying to bring people together, but somehow they do not succeed. There is a confusion, a separation. There are divisions. There are antagonisms. That is the situation with which we are confronted. Where does it come from? What is the origin of it all? And the answer is to be found in the eleventh chapter of the book of Genesis.

"Now," says someone, "wait a minute. You surely don't think that anybody today is going to accept that as history? That's folklore. You're taking us to the realm of children's storybooks. There was never really an attempt to build a Tower of Babel."

If you want to say something like that to me, my first reply to you is that you are very much behind the times in your understanding and in your scholarship. That was the sort of objection that was raised up until, say, twenty years ago. Of course, it was *the* thing to say fifty years ago because the scholars had come to the conclusion that there was practically no real history at all in the Old Testament. There may have been some at the time of the prophets, but Genesis and Exodus, of course, were not historical. They were symbolical. There never was such a person as Moses. There never was such a person as Abraham. These are idealized personages made up by clever writers to represent a certain point of view.

But there has been a very interesting change. The Old Testament has become amazingly popular. Now this is not my theory—this is a fact. The number of books that are being published on the Old Testament prove what I am saying. All the so-called scholars are agreeing that there is a new interest in the Old Testament. People are seeing how it is the key to everything, the key to the whole world situation today. And the discoveries of archaeology are one after another confirming in detail the historicity of these early chapters of Genesis. It is most astonishing. And scholars who twenty years ago would have doubted all this now accept it all as fact. They are bound to. They have the evidence of archaeology staring them in the face.

But with regard to the Tower of Babel, something else has always seemed to me to be of very great interest and extreme importance. It concerns the confusion of languages. Look at all the languages that are in the world today. Did you know that it is a fact that all this multiplicity of languages can be reduced to certain fundamental types or families? This is a most fascinating study, and I commend it to you. There are certain great groups of languages out of which many individual languages have come. You will be amazed at the correspondence between languages that on the surface seem to be entirely different. Take, for instance, the great family of languages that is sometimes called Indo-Germanic or Indo-European, out of which English and German, among others, have come. It is perfectly astonishing to see that they have a common root. It is the same with the whole group of Semitic languages and the languages to which Chinese belongs. There are certain great fundamental families of languages. Their origin cannot be traced further back than that, but you feel you have gone 75 percent of the journey back to the Tower of Babel, to a time when there was only one language, from which there was a division that spread out in all directions.

So this idea that we can avoid the message of the early chapters of the Bible no longer holds water. We have sound historical evidence on a sound historical basis. Very well, then, let us pay careful attention to the message that is given to us here. What does this story, this incident of the Tower of Babel, really teach us? I want to divide it in this way: first, I will make a general remark, and then I will come to the particulars.

The general remark is that I see in this story the whole essence of the human tragedy. We are told that the people said to one another, "Go to, let us make brick, and burn them thoroughly. And they had brick for stone, and slime had they for mortar" (Genesis 11:3). Incidentally, those details are very interesting from the standpoint of geology, from the standpoint of the difference between Palestine and Egypt, on the one hand, and this land of Shinar, as it is called, on the other hand. The land of Palestine had stones, but in Shinar the people had to make bricks when they wanted to build.

But the point to which I want to call your attention is this: do you not see here the whole tragedy of humanity? It is this. Look at these people making their bricks. They made bricks very much as bricks are still made. They took their earth, the sort of clay soil that was necessary, and shaped it into the form of bricks, which they then put into furnaces to bake, to harden them. Now how did they ever come to do that? Obviously there is only one answer. It was because people observed the effect of the heat of the sun upon clay. They saw that when the sun was beating down upon clay, it gradually hardened, becoming so hard that it was like stone. So in lands that were not blessed with quarries and a great supply of stone, the people, after observing what the sun could do, suddenly saw that they could make stones for themselves. And so brickmaking came into existence.

What a wonder man is! Think of all the discoveries people have made purely as the result of observation. Nothing is as wonderful and impressive in the story of the human race as this. It is the source of most medical treatment. Do you not sometimes wonder why certain drugs are given for specific ailments? Why is it that for some 150 years a drug called digitalis has been prescribed for heart failure? How did that come about? Well, it began because somebody observed—we do not know when—that if you make a kind of infusion of foxglove and give it to people to drink, it cures their dropsy. But how did somebody observe that? Well, there is the greatness of man. Somehow or other these observations have been made. Man, you see, has been given a mind and a brain by God. He was made in the image of God. He has extraordinary faculties and propensities, and it is in these discoveries, based on observation, that he shows them.

Take the origin of vaccinations. At a time when there were terrible and severe epidemics of smallpox, a man named Edward Jenner observed—it was pure observation—that dairymaids did not seem to fall ill with smallpox as frequently as other people. He began to wonder why, and he observed that these dairymaids were subject to a disease of the skin on their hands that they caught from the udders of the cows they milked—cowpox. So he asked the obvious question: "I wonder whether this, which looks so much like smallpox, protects those dairymaids against smallpox?"

So then Edward Jenner took the next step. "Well, I could try it out," he thought. So he took a little cowpox and scratched it into the arms of people who had never had smallpox, and he found that the cowpox was reproduced and then people did not get smallpox. Hence the discovery of vaccination. A creature who can do a thing like that is a very remarkable being. Oh, man is a great being!

The discovery of penicillin is another example. Again, this was due to a bit of observation by Sir Alexander Fleming. It was something that had always been there, but at last he saw it, and he thought about it, and he went on to make his discovery.

Now these people in that ancient time observed that the sun had a hardening effect upon the clay, and they said that was the way to make stones. "We don't have any, so we'll make them." What a wonderful creature man is! This ought to be a perfect world! Nothing should ever go wrong in a world inhabited by such people, people who are capable of these tremendous observations and deductions and experiments and inventions. Such creatures ought to know how to manage their world and themselves to perfection. They should have a world entirely free from trouble.

But I need not tell you that is not the case. Here is the whole essence of the tragedy of men and women—so great in those respects but completely failing to manage themselves and their lives and their own affairs. Yes, they can make bricks and discover digitalis, but they cannot discover how to live with themselves or with others. This fatal contradiction is there on the very surface of this account. But that, I say, is merely a general observation, and I am anxious to bring you to the particulars, because it is in the particulars that we see the essence of the teaching here.

I can put the particular message in this form: we are shown here that men and women will persist in thinking of life entirely apart from God. That is the essence of the trouble. Now how is this revealed? It is in the building of this city. The great St. Augustine put the whole history of the world in that form, did he not? He wrote a mighty book called *The City of God*. And the whole point of his book is that the history of humanity is the history of the struggle between two cities—the city of God and the city of man.

Now this goes back right to the very beginning. The first person to build a city was none other than Cain, the son of Adam and Eve, who murdered his own brother Abel. So the message at this point is that cities and civilization, which is nothing but the city idea exaggerated and magnified, are man's way of displaying his enmity against God. This is a most fascinating struggle.

How does it work out? Well, in essence it comes down to an analysis of the whole idea of civilization. *Civilization* really means people getting together to organize life in this world apart from God. And that is what they began to do in this incident of the Tower of Babel. They said, "Let's get together. Let's organize our life in one great mass."

But God had told them to do something very different: "And God blessed Noah and his sons, and said unto them, Be fruitful, and multiply, and replenish the earth" (Genesis 9:1). He wanted them to replenish the whole earth and to fill it. But they did the exact opposite. They said in effect, "No. We won't scatter. We'll all keep ourselves together. We'll build a city." Indeed, they gave that very reason for it. They said, "Go to, let us build us a city and a tower, whose top may reach unto heaven; and let us make us a name, lest we be scattered abroad upon the face of the whole earth" (Genesis 11:4). They were afraid of being scattered, and so they said they would organize all this together. And the various reasons that they gave still obtain today.

The people built their city for the sake of trade and pleasure and security. Those were the three controlling ideas. They always have been. They said, "We must have enough to eat and to drink, and we cannot have that without trading. Very well, we'll organize our trade. And then, of course, we must have our pleasures. And you can always enjoy yourself much better when you're together than when you're separated and living a long way off from one another—someone on a farm here and someone else miles away. We'll all be together and organize our pleasures. It's all going to be so wonderful. And, of course, in that life out in the country, that nomadic life, we're subject to the attacks of animals and robbers and so on. Well, let's all get together in a city. We'll be secure. We'll put a great wall around it all, and nobody will be able to touch us."

But the trouble with all this is that it is a life apart from God. It is men and women giving expression to their desire for self-sufficiency, organizing the whole thing in such a way that they feel that God is entirely unnecessary. Perhaps the simplest way for me to put all this is to quote the old saying that a life on the soil is nearer to God than a life in the city. There are people who say, "Back to nature; handle the soil; have a garden; have a plot of earth, an allotment. It will be good for you, not only good physically, but it's good to be handling the actual red or brown earth." These people say that somehow or other this brings you back to God. There are poems written about this, a sort of philosophy of the garden.

Now there is a great deal of truth in all that, more truth than we sometimes realize. The teaching of the Bible is that city life, the city outlook upon life, the civilization view of human life, is always basically opposed to God. This idea of trading with one another gives us a kind of independence. If you have a garden or if you are a farmer, you begin to pay a little attention to the weather, do you not? You say, "Well, of course, the weather's tremendously important. If it's going to be a very hard spring and very cold with a lot of frost and no rain and no sun, it's going to affect my yield." You realize that the outcome is not all in your hands. The weather is important, and God is behind the weather. But if you live in a city, you need not worry about the weather. You get your bread from the baker. It is all so organized. It is so simple. The very fact that you are living in a city and getting your bread like that, this in and of itself, without going any further—it sounds ridiculous, but it is the simple truth—is an inducement and an encouragement to forget God. It is all delivered on the doorstep. But the farmer knows that it is not all delivered on the doorstep. He is aware of other factors and forces and of his dependence upon them all. He pays great attention to them, and they make him think and ponder. And back he goes to God.

Not only that, there are many other factors at work as well. Life in the country is more leisurely than life in the town. One of the curses of town life is that we are all kept so busy that we have no time left to think about God. Is that not true? Anybody who was brought up in the country and who has come to live in the city will know that I am speaking the simple truth. If you are living a nomadic life or an agricultural life, there is more time, in the words of the poet W. H. Davies, "to stand and stare." But in cities we are all rushing madly to and from work. We have no time to think about God. We have to catch a train or there is something calling us urgently. And then in the evening pleasure is organized for us, staring us in the face—the cinema, the theater, restaurants, and so on. In the country you are not face-to-face with all that. But in the city it is calling us, enticing us—the advertisements and all the rest of it. How difficult it is to find time to pray and to read devotional books and to read the Bible. "We don't have time," we say. "We can't find the time to do these things."

And then there is this awful sense of security that we have, this feeling that because we are all huddled together we are somehow safer and are protected against wild beasts and marauders and so on. The effect of all this, you see, always has been and always will be that there is no room for God.

And that is what these people in Genesis 11 were doing. They had shut God right out. They were going to live a self-sufficient life—what you and I today tend to call a *civilized* life. And it is so-called civilization that has stood out more obviously and prominently during the last hundred years than perhaps anything else at all. The tragedy is that it is now even spreading from the city to the country. With radio and television and buses and so on, the country has become like the town; there is no longer much difference. People no longer stand and stare at nature in its glory. Even in the country they are rushing into the village or to the town to some man-made entertainment. And as a result life has become impoverished. It has become uninteresting. The sameness is appalling. We have fallen into the trap and the error into which the people who built the Tower of Babel fell.

Notice another factor that is significant here. The people said they had to build with bricks. Why? Well, the city and the tower were meant to last forever. They were to be permanent. The people were going to build a durable edifice that nothing could ever shake. It was a purely "this world" view, you see. It left God out. It left Providence out. They were going to build a city that would never be destroyed, that nothing could ever shake. They believed in the development of man. They believed in evolution in this world and realm. They had no thoughts at all of eternity. And they could see their city developing and advancing on and on. How wonderful it was going to be! And here I am just describing modern philosophy.

I also want to emphasize the element of human pride and self-sufficiency and self-confidence that is seen in all this. Listen to their words: "Go to, let us build us a city and a tower, whose top may reach unto heaven; and let us make us a name" (Genesis 11:4). Marvelous, isn't it? Here is your city and the latest propaganda and advertising, and it's all absolutely perfect. Do it! Build it! Advertise it! Get the headlines and the signs so that everybody will see and stand in admiration and wonder. Man—there is no limit to him! He can build a tower to heaven. If there is a God in heaven, well, man can put up a ladder that will take him there. He will build his city in such a way that it will not only encompass the earth but also the heavens. Nothing is impossible. No longer "Glory to God in the highest," but "Glory to man in the highest." No height is too great for him. He has it in him to get anywhere. Nothing can stop him.

Is that not it? Inventions. Discoveries. Progress. Harnessing the forces of nature. Splitting the atom. Nothing can ever frustrate human beings or put a limit or a ceiling to their greatness, and they know it. There is no doubt about it. They said, "Very well, let's prove that we can do it. And we'll write our names over it all. We'll bow down and worship ourselves in our greatness and uniqueness."

Is it not obvious that I am describing to you in Old Testament terms what has been happening during the last hundred years? We decided about that time, when Charles Darwin wrote *The Origin of Species*, that there was no God. He was not necessary. We were going to do it all, and we could do it all. And we have been doing it ever since. Getting together. Organizing it all. God does not come into the picture. He is not necessary. We are going to do everything. Oh, the confidence of man in man. We were going to abolish war. We were going to turn swords into plowshares. We were going to usher in "the parliament of man" and the federation of the world. We were very certain of it at the end of the First World War. The League of Nations began, and we said, "At last we have world government! How wonderful we are! There is nothing we cannot do." This is the story of our age and of our civilization right up to today.

But at the same time men and women had a haunting sense of fear. They said, "Go to, let us build us a city and a tower, whose top may reach unto heaven; and let us make us a name, lest we be scattered abroad upon the face of the whole earth." That is great material for a preacher. Even in the height of confidence men and women always have a lurking fear. There is always a perhaps, a what if or perchance. Just when we are safest, something always seems to happen. So we take security measures. We sort of underwrite it all. We take out an insurance policy. There was the threat of being scattered, and it is still there. It always has been there. You cannot help but feel that a good deal of our whistling and singing is merely designed to keep up our courage in some awful darkness of which we are terrified.

Men and women have the recollection and the memory that God has told them, "You are not to come together in your city and be independent of me. You are to replenish the whole earth. You are to be scattered abroad. You are to be where I want you to be." The memory has remained, and the fear has ever persisted.

Nevertheless, they did it, as they did so many times afterward, and as men and women have been doing with all their might in this century. But what happens?

And the LORD came down to see the city and the tower, which the children of men builded. And the LORD said, Behold, the people is one, and they have all one language; and this they begin to do: and now nothing will be restrained from them, which they have imagined to do. Go to, let us go down, and there confound their language, that they may not understand one another's speech. So the LORD scattered them abroad from thence upon the face of all the earth: and they left off to build the city. (vv. 5-8)

That literally happened. God looked down upon all this, and he knew exactly what was happening. He saw the rebellion and the arrogance, the independence and the hatred of himself. And he looked down, and he came down, and he caused that confusion of language. He scattered the people abroad throughout the whole earth.

My dear friend, God always does that, and he has pledged that he always will. This is not the only time he did it. He did exactly the same thing with a great city called Nineveh. What a marvelous city! It was the capital city of a glorious civilization but godless—and it was completely destroyed. It has entirely vanished. God did the same thing with Babylon. That nation was so great that its king, Nebuchadnezzar, had an image made of himself and asked people to bow down and worship him as the conqueror of the whole earth, the man who in his might had unified everything. It is now all gone. It has vanished completely. The same thing happened with Greece and with Rome.

God has never tolerated this idea that man could build a city in any shape or form that was independent of him. Any nation that has been foolish enough to imagine itself to be a world conqueror has always been smashed and destroyed. That is why some of us at the height of Hitlerism were not at all terrified about the ultimate result. We knew it could not persist. Whether it be the British Empire or any other empire, it shall not establish itself like this. God will not allow it. So we have seen these kingdoms going down one after another. And let me say this: if all the nations today decide to surrender their sovereignty and to join together to form a great world state and to set up a unified government of man, precisely the same will happen to that. God will not tolerate it.

God came down, and he confused them, and he scattered them. Why? In order to punish their sin; to tell them, "There is no peace . . . to the wicked" (Isaiah 57:21); to say that though you build your great city and put a mighty wall around it, it will not be safe if it is not under God. The walls will be smashed. The enemy will come rushing in. And all that you have built will suddenly come to an end.

God confused their language to punish the people, but not only that. As we are told here, he also did it to restrain them. God looked down and said in essence, "They have started building this tower to heaven. If we do not go down and interrupt it and spoil it, nothing will hold them back, nothing will restrain them. So let us go down and stop it now."

And God has been doing that throughout the running centuries. To me this is the only explanation of the history of this present [twentieth] century with its two devastating world wars. At the end of the last century and the beginning of this, we were absolutely confident that we were going to outlaw war. We were going to produce a world in which we would all be doing nothing but eating and drinking and enjoying ourselves. Science would have developed so marvelously that nobody would need to work at all. You would press a button and your meal would arrive. The whole world was going to be perfect. With our inventions we would have perpetual enjoyment and entertainment. Even if we were working, we would be singing. What a picture—God left out of it all, people living for themselves. But we have not had that. We have had wars instead, and bloodshed and terror and alarm and disappointment and misery. And I do not hesitate to assert that God is at the back of it. It is God, I say, causing this confusion in order to restrain men from a final assertion of themselves, which would lead again to world destruction as at the Flood. It was a means of restraint.

And, of course, God's other reason was that he might bring

to pass the command that he had given to Noah and his children, namely, to replenish the whole earth, to be scattered over the whole world. God brings his purpose to pass in spite of us when we refuse to act at his command. And God is still the same. In other words, the great lesson of this eleventh chapter of Genesis, the lesson of the Tower of Babel, is just this: people in sin are fools. They think they can defy Almighty God. They lay their plans without remembering him. They turn their backs upon God. They carry on. They begin to build. The tower goes up. Then suddenly God comes down, and it is all destroyed.

My dear friend, this is true not only of nations but of the individual. What is your view of life today? We are all expert planners, are we not? Those people were planners. They drew the specifications of the city. They had it all worked out. We all do that in life, do we not? You have your plans. Your future life and career are mapped out. You know what you want to do. Where does God come in? Is the plan made under God, or is it made apart from him? The one lesson of this chapter is that if you plan your life without God at the center, it will come to nothing, nothing at all. It will be as futile and as fatuous as the Tower of Babel. God will come down and will destroy it, whether you like that or not. This is the whole history of the Bible. It is the history of the subsequent centuries after the end of the Bible. It is the history of the twentieth century. The human race is not allowed to build a civilization without God, and you are not allowed to build your life without God.

There is only one way of unity. There is only one way of understanding, one way of peace and joy. We see it in the second chapter of Acts where many different races and nations and peoples said, "We do hear them speak in our tongues the wonderful works of God" (v. 11). That was Pentecost, the power of the Holy Spirit. What does it mean? It means there is only one point at which men and women can be brought together and legitimately be made one—in Christ, in God.

We are all one in sin. We are all lost. We need the same salvation, and we are confronted by the same Savior. The whole world becomes one in its need. It all looks up to God, and God gives his salvation and his Holy Spirit. When humanity realizes its sin, when we all realize individually that we are sinners and under the wrath of God and are hopeless and helpless, we cease to be jealous and envious and enemies. We all drop down on our knees, and we find our enemy on his knees by our side. The middle wall of partition is broken down in Christ. The differences are abolished, and a new unity comes into being. People begin to love one another. Why? Because now they have the Spirit of the living God within them.

The tragedy today is that the world is ignoring this message and trying in the old futile method of the Tower of Babel to do what can never be done. My dear friend, are you at peace within? Are you at peace with others? How are your plans going? What is happening to you? Have you faced all the eventualities and possibilities? Are you living your life under God, realizing that the supreme thing in life is to be blessed by him, that unless God blesses, all is in vain, but if God blesses, all is well?

Is God blessing you? Do you know that for certain? If not, it is because you planned without him. But if you have done that, recognize it now. Repent. Confess it. Fly to God in acknowledgment of your godlessness, your arrogance, your pride, your folly, your enmity. Fall down before him in penitence and in contrition. And as you do, he will certainly assure you that he sent his own Son to die for you and for your sins. He will pardon you and forgive you. He will give you a new life and a new spirit. You will have a new understanding and a new outlook, and you will understand others and will be at peace with yourself and with others. And you will go out to live life in a new way with your eye upon a new city, "a city which hath foundations, whose builder and maker is God" (Hebrews 11:10), the city of God.

9

ABRAHAM:
THE LIFE OF FAITH

Now the LORD had said unto Abram, Get thee out of thy coun-
try, and from thy kindred, and from thy father's house, unto
a land that I will show thee: And I will make of thee a great
nation, and I will bless thee, and make thy name great; and
thou shalt be a blessing: And I will bless them that bless thee,
and curse him that curseth thee: and in thee shall all families
of the earth be blessed. So Abram departed, as the LORD had
spoken unto him.

GENESIS 12:1-4

We are continuing this series of studies with regard to the whole question of what the Bible has to say to us about our lives in this world. Our object is to show that the criticism, which, alas, is so common, that the Bible is a book that is remote from life and has nothing much to say to us in this modern world is based upon nothing but sheer ignorance. Our purpose is to show that the Bible is the most practical and up-to-date book in the world and that its interest is not in some theoretical religion but in the practical business of life and living. The Bible, in other words, makes no less a claim than this: it is a book from God, and it is God who has there revealed himself, has revealed us to ourselves, and has revealed the cause of our troubles and the only possible cure for all our ills. And that is why, among a great deal of doctrine, we have also a great deal of history in that book. The Bible tells us that God has actually intervened in the life of this world.

The position can be summarized like this: The world has been made by God. There is the essential beginning. This world has not just come into being somehow. We dealt with that point in particular in our first study. Of course, this is an obvious point of division. You either believe that this world has been made by God, or you are prepared to believe the current, so-called scientific teaching that really does not explain, because it cannot, but merely postulates that the whole cosmos as we know it has come into being in a purely accidental manner. This unbiblical teaching declares that man with his wonderful gifts and propensities and extraordinary talents that we all possess is the product of pure accident, absolute chance, and there is no rhyme or reason, no purpose, no design to the universe. Obviously there, at the very outset, we see a fundamental difference in belief about the world.

Now the Bible says, you see, that the world has been made by God and that men and women have been made by God and made in the image of God and made in such a way that they can only live full and happy lives as long as they are true to the law of their beings and as long as they are in relationship with God.

But the message goes on to tell us that in their folly Adam and Eve turned their backs against all that. They sinned. They rebelled against God. They accepted the suggestion that God was against them, and they tried to assert themselves and make themselves equal with God, and thereby they fell. And all the troubles with the world ever since, right up to today and including today, are the direct outcome of that one act. The world is as it is because of sin, because men and women have become alienated from God, because they have been trying to live independent lives. That act of rebellion produced immediate chaos, and the chaos has continued.

And, of course, Adam and Eve received God's judgment. God punished them. God thrust them out of the garden, out of paradise, and made it impossible for them to go back in their own strength.

And thus their troubles began. They had to start earning their bread by the sweat of their brow. They had problems to contend with, thorns and thistles and briars. Disease and pestilence and so on came in. We have seen that by the time of Noah, sin was so rampant that God announced that he was going to destroy the world, and he did so in a flood. Only eight people were saved in the ark. God had visited punishment upon sin in order to make the truth clear.

Then there was a new beginning. But we have seen that after a very brief time, looked at from the standpoint of world history, the human race had gone back again into the same old position. Men and women decided to build themselves a great city with a tower going up to heaven. They organized themselves in the form of city life and tried to produce what may be called a civilization, rendering themselves quite independent of God in every respect whatsoever and enabling them to assert themselves. They turned into a kind of mutual admiration society. They did it and boasted of it and put up their great name.

And we saw that God again visited the people with punishment. God came down and confused their language, and they had to leave their tower, and their city disappeared. God punished them, as he had said he would, and they were scattered over the whole earth.

That is the position at which we have arrived, and now we come to the twelfth chapter of the book of Genesis. In many ways this is, of course, one of the most important points in the history of the entire human race. It is a part of the same plan that God had announced way back in the garden of Eden. He made the announcement, you remember, that there would be warfare between the seed of the woman and the seed of the serpent. He announced it, and it has happened ever since. There has been this perpetual struggle between God's people and those who belong to the world and ignore God. But here we come to one of the most important and vital turning points of all.

Three times over God had allowed humanity to see what it could do in and of itself. He had allowed this when he first created man, then again after man fell, leading up to the Flood, and again after the Flood. Three times over, as it were, God faced the whole of humanity, and having given his law and having given his punishment because of the breaking of the law, he waited, as it were, to see what they would do. And as I have reminded you, they persisted in their evil course.

But now God took a new and a special action. He announced that he was going to do something quite different, that he was going to start a different type of life. He was going to form a people for himself and to himself. And he proceeded to do it in the call of this man Abraham (first called Abram). The story of Abraham is absolutely pivotal in any understanding of the whole message of the Bible. The essence of the message, I would remind you again, is that once man sinned, he put himself under the power and influence and dominion of the Devil, who since then has been controlling the life of this world. But now God came in and made this other seed, this other people.

In Abraham God formed a new nation, a nation unto himself, a separate people through whom he was going to further his own great plan and purpose. So the call of Abraham is something that we must understand if we really want to grasp what the Bible tells us with regard to the possibilities confronting us at this moment. We are all aware of the state of the world. But the question is, are we aware of the other possibility? The fact is, God *is* announcing another possibility. Another type of life is possible to us in this world—a life given by God, a life in communion with God, a life under the blessing of God. We see that the godless life leads to misery and turmoil and wretchedness and finally brings down the judgment of God. But here is a life that is absolutely different. This is the life that is offered to us through the message of the Bible. And it is all perfectly summarized, it seems to me, in the case of this man Abraham.

The Bible constantly refers to Abraham. There are frequent references to him in both the Old and New Testaments. Abraham is "the friend of God," that is his title (Isaiah 41:8; James 2:23). Here is a man who walked with God and lived in the presence of God and who stands out as one of the noblest characters that the world has ever seen. I once heard a man describing Abraham as the greatest gentleman of all time, and I am prepared to agree with his verdict. There is no nobler, no more majestic, no more lovable character than this man Abraham, the friend of God. And what a wonderful life he lived.

The whole point is that the call of Abraham should concern us because God is calling us to the same type of life. We can be friends of God. The New Testament tells us that Abraham is the father of all the faithful (Galatians 3:6–9). Christians are described in the New Testament as "Abraham's seed" (Galatians 3:29). We are the children of Abraham because we are the children of faith. A Christian is someone who has done, in effect, the very thing that Abraham did. And, therefore, what can be more important for us than to discover what this is, because it is an essential part of the message of the Bible to say that the conditions of this life are exactly the same at this moment as they were in the days of Abraham. That is why, in the eleventh chapter of Hebrews, the author, who is writing to Christian people and wants to strengthen them and to help them because they are faced with difficulties, says in effect, "You must walk and live in this life exactly as Abraham did" (Hebrews 11:8–19). The writer has already mentioned Noah and Abel and will go on to talk about Moses and others. All these people were living the same type of life—this different, this godly life. And this is the life that is offered to us in the gospel of our Lord and Savior, Jesus Christ.

So here is the great question for us: are we living this kind of life? Are we viewing everything as Abraham did? Do we have the same confidence that he had? Do we have the same joy? Do we have the same experiences?

Or let me ask my second question: is this not the kind of life you would like to live? Abraham's world was exactly like our world. Things like planes and cars, of course, do not matter at all. They are mere incidentals. That is not life. Life was exactly the same for Abraham and his contemporaries as it is for us. The tragedy is that so many people, because of the superficial and unimportant differences, imagine that life itself is different today. People think it is monstrous to say that life now is identical to life in the time of Abraham. They say that cannot be because Abraham did not have a car, he could not fly in a plane, he did not know about the splitting of the atom. But what is life? The moment you answer that question, you discover that there is no change at all.

The only difference between the age of Abraham and today is the rate at which we do the things they did. What did people do in the time of Abraham? They ate and they drank. They made love and they made war. The only difference is that they traveled on foot or camel instead of by car or plane. The unutterable superficiality of this age to which you and I belong is that because we rush about in a semi-lunatic manner, we say how superior we are, how different.

Read this story of Abraham, and you will see modern life there. You will see how other people coveted his wife and all the troubles to which that led. That is still happening today. There is no difference. We have the same circumstances, the same world, the same difficulties. And yet here is a man who stands out. He overcame it all. He lived like a giant. He lived like a nobleman, the friend of God. That is the life to live.

So how does one live a life like that? What are the conditions? Follow this man's story and this is what you find.

Abraham lived in a pagan land, and he had been brought up as a pagan. The people worshipped a multiplicity of gods. And there he was, living with the rest. But this is what I read: "Now the LORD had said unto Abram, Get thee out of thy country, and from thy kindred, and from thy father's house, unto a land that I will show thee" (Genesis 12:1). God spoke to him. God disturbed him. God called him out. That is always, invariably, the first step. Go right through the Bible, and you will find it everywhere. Read it in the New Testament as well as the Old. Pick up any biography of any saint who has ever lived, anyone who has ever adorned the life of the church. You will find them all saying the same thing in some shape or form. They say, "There I was, living my life, doing the same things as everybody else, when suddenly (or gradually; it does not matter which) I became conscious of something that was disturbing me, something that was calling me. I felt I heard a call."

Now I could go to great lengths to point out to you the various ways in which that call comes. Sometimes it is almost indefinable. Within our feelings and our consciousness we begin to have a sense of restlessness. We have been living a certain kind of life, and we have always thought it marvelous and thrilling. Everybody else is living in the same way, and we expected that life to go on endlessly. But somehow or other we begin to feel that, well, it is not as wonderful as we had thought. We do not seem to get the same kick or the same thrill out of it. This life begins to lose its glamour, and we start to wonder what there is in it, after all. We do not know why these thoughts have come, but they have. We just find ourselves looking at things in a different way. What is this? It is the call of God. He has put different ideas into our mind. He has created a disturbance. Have you not known something about that? You begin to ask questions. Your world is shaken, and something happens.

Or God's call may come through circumstances. It can happen through an accident. It can happen through an illness. It can happen through a disappointment or a business loss or someone's death. There are a thousand and one ways in which it happens. What is important is that it happens. The even tenor of your days is disturbed, and you are stopped, and you are made to think, and you begin to ask questions. That is what happened to Abraham.

God does not always speak with an audible voice. He very rarely does in these modern times—it is not necessary because we have his Word. But God does speak to us, as I have indicated, in the unconscious or through events and circumstances entirely outside our control. How many men, how many women have said they would have gone on as far as they could see, absolutely endlessly, along a certain line, but something happened, and the whole course of their life was changed. Through circumstances or through what they would even call chance, the word and the voice and the call of God came to them.

God's call has come to many through the Bible itself. We may have read the Word thousands of times, as a matter of duty, without seeing very much in it, reading it just because we had been brought up to do so and wanted to keep a pledge or a vow made to our father or mother, and it had never spoken to us. But suddenly one day the Word seemed to stand out and was speaking to us directly, a personal word out of the Scripture.

Or God's call may come when someone is preaching or through the words of a hymn. It may be vague and indefinite. It does not matter. The great thing is that a man or woman living a certain kind of life hears the word of God, the call of God.

You know this, I take it. You know what it is to be unhappy because of your life. You know what it is, do you not, to pause and to query and to question. Maybe you have left your youth behind you. Perhaps you are coming into middle age, and the elasticity is going out of your life a bit. You may be even older. You may be realizing that your time in this life is now very short, and the end may come, and you do not know much about what is going to happen beyond it. In these various ways we are brought short, and we are called.

But that call is not merely general—it is a specific call. Notice the specific call in the case of Abraham. "Get thee out of thy country, and from thy kindred, and from thy father's house." What does this mean? Well, in many ways I think this is perhaps the most interesting part of it all. Abraham was told to separate himself from all that had hitherto been his life. He was told to leave that pagan atmosphere. He had to leave the country and his kindred. He had to leave everything. He had to come right out of it and go into something else.

I want to try to show you the interesting way in which this

account follows upon the account of those people in Genesis 11 who set to work to build a city and their Tower of Babel. There is the kind of life in which Abraham had been brought up, a life, as I have told you, of independence from God, a life in which people build a city and form a so-called civilization. Remember in particular the emphasis that was placed upon their words, "Let us make us a name" (v. 4). They baked their bricks. They put them together with mortar. Their city was meant to last forever. They were going to settle down to live in this world. They did not consider God. God was not necessary at all. They planned to live a self-sufficient city life and make a great name for themselves.

And Abraham was called entirely out of that sort of life. In other words, the specific call that comes to every one of us is the call to repentance. What Abraham was asked to do by God was this: he was to look at the kind of life that he was living and see that it was wrong and that he must therefore come out of it. That is what the Bible calls repentance. It means that we are made to think again about the type of life we are living. We suddenly take a look at this civilization, this city life that is entirely independent of God. We are asked really to look at it and to understand it and to see where it leads. And then when we have seen it, we are asked to confess that it is all wrong and to turn our backs upon it and to come out of it and to go away and do the exact opposite.

That is what repentance means. Having paused to think and to consider, we now come to see that the kind of life and existence we have been living is a life that is utterly dishonoring to God. God did not come into our thoughts, into our calculations, at all. We had made that life ourselves. We had manufactured it. We had thought it. We had brought it into being. We had been interested in ourselves and in ourselves alone. Glorifying ourselves. Making ourselves into gods. Doing things and then admiring them—and the whole world was doing the same thing with us.

But the moment we are dealt with by the Spirit of God, the moment this call of God comes, we begin to realize that our life is without a foundation. We see that it is a transient, evanescent, pass-ing life. It is not durable. We can see that what we had regarded as so solid is not really solid at all, that civilizations are smashed and come and go and that we ourselves, in any case, will soon have to leave it all behind. And then we begin to think that there was no basis at all in our life. We have been living for things that cannot satisfy. And so we begin to hear this tremendous call from God to come out of all this and to recognize its sinfulness and the folly of thinking that people should try to live in this world apart from God who made them and who has made their whole world, the God who visits punishment on sin.

We suddenly become awakened to all this. We realize that sort of life cannot satisfy a living soul, that it always leads to confusion and uncertainty, to unhappiness and misery, to jealousy and envy and pride and spite and malice. We see it quite clearly. We see now that the whole cause of our trouble is that people do not base their lives upon God. They have set themselves up as gods, and the gods are fighting one another, and life has become chaos. So we turn to God and confess it all. We admit our folly. We admit our failure. We admit our arrogance, our rebellion against God. We acknowledge that we deserve nothing but punishment, that we have lived like that in spite of the Bible. We have done it all in spite of the fact that God's own Son came into this world to call us from that sort of life and even died upon the cross in order that we might be delivered from it. We realize that we have lived in ignorance and blindness in spite of all this. And we acknowledge it all to God and realize that we can do nothing but cry out to God for mercy and compassion. We thank God that we are awakened and that he has called us to this realization. Like Abraham of old, we hear the call to come out of that civilized life, so called, that is so terribly and violently opposed to God.

And then what happens? We face God's positive proposal. Here it is in these words to Abraham. He is told to come out of his coun-try and from his kindred and from his father's house, to go where?

". . . unto a land that I will show thee: and I will make of thee a great nation, and I will bless thee, and make thy name great; and thou shalt be a blessing."

Here we come back to something I mentioned when we were considering the Tower of Babel. The Bible puts its case in a contrasting form. On the one hand, men and women make their city, they want to make a great name for themselves; and on the other hand, God has his proposal, his offer. Notice what God offers: it is the very thing that the people had been trying to get for themselves. God offers to make Abraham's name great. People are always trying to make a name for themselves, and it always comes to nothing. But God offers to make Abraham's name a great name. And he offers him the blessings and the prosperity and, indeed, the city that people desire.

Now that is a pictorial way of putting it all. But all of us either have our eye on the city of man or on the city of God. That is the difference between people who are not Christians and those who are. It is all a question of whether we are trying to make ourselves great or whether we realize that God alone can give us greatness through adopting us into his family. We are either trying to build our self-sufficient civilization or we realize that we must wait upon God to be blessed by him. It is one or the other. But this is what God offers. He offers us this blessing, this wonderful name, this other city, the city of God, not the city of the world—the eternal city, not the city of time.

Now all this, of course, is offered to us much more clearly and plainly than it was to Abraham. But Abraham saw it afar off. You remember the words of the Lord Jesus Christ. He said one afternoon, "Your father Abraham rejoiced to see my day: and he saw it, and was glad" (John 8:56). God spoke to him, and Abraham saw what was coming. We do not have a complete record of it here, but God told him that out of his loins, out of his seed, would come the final Messiah and Deliverer, the One who would deliver the mortal blow to the serpent and all his seed. And in a sense the whole history of the Old Testament is just the history of the development of this seed of Abraham, starting with one man and his wife and a child named Isaac and the children of Isaac and on and on and on right down the centuries until at last you come to a baby born in Bethlehem. This baby is the seed of Abraham; he is a son of Abraham. Here the promise is fulfilled, the promise that God had revealed vaguely to Abraham, that Abraham had seen afar off.

Abraham saw more. You remember that he was commanded one day to take his son Isaac, the son of promise, and to kill him as an offering to God (Genesis 22). Indeed, he had raised his hand to do just that when God stopped him and told him that he had provided a ram for the sacrifice. And there Abraham saw—in a very indistinct way, but nevertheless he saw—that what he had been asked to do and then had been stopped from doing, God was going to do with his only Son, born after the flesh of the seed of Abraham, in order that mankind might be delivered.

In other words, my friends, in this we see the offer of the gospel. God comes to us through his Holy Spirit and disturbs us and convicts us in the way that I have been trying to show you. Then he puts before us this other kind of life, this life that is related to him, this life in which we are granted forgiveness for all our sin and folly, this life in which we are given a new life from the Son of God himself and the power of the Spirit. And we are given a new name—yes, the name "children of God . . . heirs of God, and joint-heirs with Christ" (Romans 8:16–17). We are adopted into God's family. "I will bless thee, and make thy name great" (Genesis 12:2). God put a new name, as it were, upon Abraham—"the friend of God," the one through whom the whole world would be blessed.

And that is the offer of the Christian message to every one of us. Another type of life is possible. Not a life of uncertainty based upon our own powers and upon the world, but an unseen life that is based upon God, a life that gives us peace with God and peace within, knowledge of sins forgiven, a new outlook upon life, an entirely new life with new strength and power.

That was the offer that was made to Abraham. Come out— go in.

Now at this point, of course, the only thing that matters is what we do about this. That was the critical moment for Abraham. God had spoken to him to come out. What would he do? And the answer is that Abraham believed God. That is what the Scriptures tell us about him: "Abraham believed God, and it was accounted to him for righteousness" (Galatians 3:6). He went out and did it all. On what basis? Simply on the bare word of God and nothing else at all. He had nothing but the word of God that had been spoken to him. He had no proof. He could not demonstrate it on paper. Probably his relatives argued with him and remonstrated with him and said, "Where are you going? We've always lived in this district. You're leaving society. You're leaving civilization. You're going to live in tents. You're going to be a sojourner, a traveler. Are you mad? Why? What can you prove?"

And Abraham could only say, "I have nothing but the word of the living God, and I'm ready to act upon it." He believed entirely and solely because God called him to do so.

Faith means believing the word of God. It means that I believe what God tells me about that other kind of life in this world. What is my view of that life? Do I take my view from the newspapers or from the Bible? What do I think of the world and its whole organization? Do I know that the world as it is apart from God is under the wrath of God and is going to be destroyed? Abraham was told that, and he believed it.

On the other hand, Abraham was told that there was this other life, which he could enter here and now. It might be the life of a sojourner in this world, he might have to live in tents with his children, but he was going to God. He was right with God. God would bless him. God would prosper him. He had nothing to show but this bare word of God. Would he or would he not believe it? Faith says, "I believe because it's God who's speaking." And Abraham believed God.

The whole question for us at this moment is whether we believe God. The gospel puts it in utter simplicity. It tells us and asks us to believe that "God so loved the world, that he gave his only begotten Son, that whosoever believeth in him should not perish, but have everlasting life" (John 3:16).

"Can you prove to me," says someone, "that Jesus of Nazareth was the Son of God?"

I cannot prove it to you as a theory, as a geometrical problem. I cannot establish it in the sense that I can give you a mathematical proof. But I have God's Word, which describes him, which puts him before me. Son of God, Son of man—here is the record—the Word of God. And I believe it. It tells me that to forsake everything else and to follow him and to trust myself to him entirely will lead me to be blessed of God. And faith believes that. It simply takes it on the word of the almighty God. It simply believes him.

People bring forward their objections, their supposed scientific and other objections. They say they do not understand miracles. But that is the opposite of faith. There is nothing unreasonable about faith. Once you believe it, you see the reasons for it. It all begins to work itself out before your wondering gaze. But at first you have nothing but this bare word of God. And on that Abraham acted. Faith—belief—obedience.

And obedience, of course, is an essential part of faith. What a wonderful way the Scriptures put it. We are told, "So Abram departed, as the LORD had spoken unto him" (Genesis 12:4). Abraham acted on this word of God. Having believed it, he went out. I think this is one of the most magnificent statements in the Bible. Did you notice how the eleventh chapter of Hebrews puts it? "And he went out, not knowing whither he went" (v. 8). Though he did not know where he was going, he went. I rather like the comment of an old Puritan of three hundred years ago on that. He said, "Abraham went out not knowing whither he went, but he did know with whom he was going." That is the very essence of faith—you risk, you bank, your all upon the Lord Jesus Christ.

Notice the other way in which this is put in the eleventh chapter of Hebrews. This is the whole essence of this matter. We are told that these people, Abraham among them, regarded themselves as "strangers and pilgrims on the earth" (v. 13). Abraham said farewell forever to the Babel view of life, to the society of the city, to life in this world with its bricks and mortar and people glorifying themselves, for he said this was not the only world. This was a passing world, a dying world, and he was a traveler and a sojourner, a pilgrim and a stranger. He was going out of cities to live in a tent to remind himself that life and reality awaited him.

Do you see what a contrast this is to that other view? It is an essential part of faith to obey God in that way. This does not, of course, mean that in a literal sense you have to go out of life or out of business or out of a profession and become a traveler. But it means that in a spiritual sense you definitely do so. And if until tonight you have been living for your business or for your profession, you must stop doing that. You say, "That's transient; that's temporary. That's not me. That's not my life. From now on I'm hanging loosely to that. I'm a stranger. I'm not building here forever. My building is over there, wherever God leads." You realize that you are a stranger and a pilgrim in this world, and far from always doing your utmost to banish thoughts of death and the grave, you deliberately face them. You deliberately look at this world and see how passing it is. And you say, "Of course it is, and I don't belong to it any longer. I'm in it, but I'm not of it. I will come out of it; I *have* come out of it."

I like another way in which this is put in that eleventh chapter of Hebrews: "[Abraham] looked for a city which hath foundations, whose builder and maker is God" (v. 10). The other city men said, "Go to, let us build us a city." They were the makers. They laid the foundations. They were everything. It was always man. But Abraham said in essence, "No, no. That's not the sort of city I want." God can blow upon such a city. An earthquake can reduce that to rubble in a moment. An atomic bomb can smash dozens of them in one go. That's not a durable city. The city that I'm seeking and that I'm heading for is a city that's founded on the Rock of Ages, whose builder and maker is not man but God himself. God is the architect, the planner, the builder. There is a city that will never be destroyed, that can never be shaken—the city of God.

So Abraham went out, keeping his eye on that land for which he was headed. This is only a tent life. That is the eternal life.

My dear friends, we are only in this world for about seventy years—perhaps for some people a little more. This is a passing world. Beyond death, beyond life in this world, beyond the grave is eternity. That is where we are heading. Life on earth is but a preparatory school. We are here today and gone tomorrow. "Change and decay in all around I see."[8] But the next life is everlasting, and that is where we should be looking. That is the reality.

Abraham was ready to endure anything. He let Lot, his nephew, choose the marvelous cities of the plain and the fruitful valley and put his cattle and sheep there. Abraham remained on the tops of the mountains. That did not trouble him. He was still looking beyond. Read his story for yourself, and you will find that he always did that. He spent much of his time, the record tells us, building altars, glorifying God. Even when God tested him by asking him to kill his son Isaac, the son of the promise, Abraham was ready to do it. Why? Because he knew that God could bring Isaac back from the dead if he wanted to. He believed God to that extent (Hebrews 11:19).

That is faith, faith that manifests itself in constant obedience. And because Abraham did just that, he was the friend of God, the greatest gentleman of history, the noble soul that he was, walking like a giant through this world of sin, living a triumphant life.

My dear friend, though you and I are living many centuries after Abraham, would you not like to live as Abraham lived? Would you not like to be able to look at death and beyond as Abraham did? I have told you the secret. Believe what God says about life as it is apart from him, and come out of it. It will never satisfy you, it will always lead to misery, and in the end it will lead to death and the judgment of God through all eternity. Come out of it. Listen to the call of God to follow Jesus Christ. God forgives your sin and folly. Christ endured the punishment for your sin, and God gives you free pardon. He will give you a new name, the name of his own Son. And he will lead you through life, through death, and even into the eternal city itself with all its everlasting bliss and joy.

NOTES

1. Alfred Tennyson, "In Memoriam."
2. William Wordsworth, "The World Is Too Much with Us."
3. Alexander Pope, "Know Thyself."
4. William Wordsworth, "Laodamia."
5. Oswald Allen, "Today Thy Mercy Calls Us."
6. Augustus Toplady, "A Debtor to Mercy Alone."
7. Armistice Sunday, an international holiday, is observed in commemoration of the end of World War I.
8. Henry Francis Lyte, "Abide with Me."